The Sustainability
Mindset

The Sustainability Mindset

Using the Matrix Map to Make Strategic Decisions

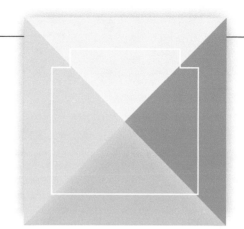

Steve Zimmerman
Jeanne Bell

JB JOSSEY-BASS™
A Wiley Brand

Cover design: C. Wallace

Cover photograph: Defocused Lights © iStock.com/gordana jovanovic

Published by Jossey-Bass

A Wiley Brand

One Montgomery Street, Suite 1200, San Francisco, CA 94104-4594—www.josseybass.com

Jossey-Bass books and products are available through most bookstores. To contact Jossey-Bass directly call our Customer Care Department within the U.S. at 800-956-7739, outside the U.S. at 317-572-3986, or fax 317-572-4002.

Wiley publishes in a variety of print and electronic formats and by print-on-demand. Some material included with standard print versions of this book may not be included in e-books or in print-on-demand. If this book refers to media such as a CD or DVD that is not included in the version you purchased, you may download this material at http://booksupport.wiley.com. For more information about Wiley products, visit www.wiley.com.

Library of Congress Cataloging-in-Publication Data

Zimmerman, Steve, 1970–

   The sustainability mindset : using the matrix map to make strategic decisions / Steve Zimmerman, Jeanne Bell.

     1 online resource.

   Includes index.

   Description based on print version record and CIP data provided by publisher; resource not viewed.

   ISBN 978-1-118-76724-5 (pdf); ISBN 978-1-118-76731-3 (epub); ISBN 978-1-118-76735-1 (paperback)

  1. Nonprofit organizations—Finance.   2. Nonprofit organizations—Management.   3. Strategic planning. I.   Bell, Jeanne, 1969- II.   Title.

  HD62.6

  658.4'012—dc23

2014024684

FIRST EDITION

PB Printing   10 9 8 7 6 5 4 3 2 1

Contents

Figures, Tables, Exhibits, and Templates

Figures

Tables

Exhibits

Templates

Acknowledgments

Our work with the matrix map as a tool to better understand nonprofit business models and drive nonprofit strategy has been influenced by many who work diligently and tirelessly to support communities and nonprofits. The tool itself is an adaption of the Growth-Share Matrix, originally developed by the Boston Consulting Group and sometimes known as the BCG matrix.

We are grateful for the long-time partnership of Jan Masaoka, our coauthor on *Nonprofit Sustainability*, in spreading and testing the core concepts that formed the basis for this follow-up book. We also acknowledge the input of Shannon Ellis of the CompassPoint practice. As a partner to Jeanne in CompassPoint's evolving strategy work with clients and a reader of early drafts of this book, she made invaluable contributions to this book's framing and clarity.

Finally, we're humbled by the outpouring of support and enthusiasm we received for *Nonprofit Sustainability* and the matrix map from clients and nonprofit professionals across the country. We have listened and incorporated your comments, suggestions, and feedback, and we believe they've resulted in a more rigorous and beneficial tool. Thank you for your encouragement and, more important, the significant work you do every day in our communities.

Steve Zimmerman
Milwaukee, Wisconsin
Jeanne Bell
Oakland, California

The Sustainability Mindset

Introduction

In the five years since we wrote *Nonprofit Sustainability*, we've had the opportunity to share the book's core messages about strategy formation and the matrix map tool for nonprofit business model analysis with thousands of nonprofit leaders across the country and internationally.[1] So today, we have a much deeper understanding of how and why the tool is a powerful catalyst for change in an organization—how, for instance, it can support a staff and board in deciding to end the "untouchable" program that hasn't been relevant for years and bring leaders to acknowledge that their fundraising programs don't yield sufficient surplus to subsidize their government funding—and get them talking honestly about what to do about it. Indeed over the past five years, the matrix map process has ignited candid self-reflection and bold decision making in organizations of all types and sizes, from direct service, to advocacy, to the arts.

While the matrix map tool is meant for episodic analyses of the strengths and weaknesses of a nonprofit's current business model, the thinking that undergirds it is essential for leaders to promote every day across their staffs and boards. It is a mindset that examines both the mission impact and the economics of a given strategy or decision. It is a mindset that does not pit these two forces against one another but instead holds them as powerfully interdependent. It is a mindset we call the *sustainability mindset*.

Definition

"Sustainability encompasses both *financial sustainability* (the ability to generate resources to meet the needs of the present without compromising the future) and *programmatic sustainability* (the ability to develop, mature, and cycle out programs to be responsive to constituencies over time)."[2]

Defining Nonprofit Sustainability

The definition we offered in our previous book of *sustainability* for nonprofits as shown in the sidebar, holds true today.

This definition does not encompass two separate, complementary ideas. Rather, the two ideas are of one piece and are not independent of one another over time. Great organizations develop, mature, and innovate their mission-specific programs in concert with the continuous development, maturation, and innovation of their fund development programs. Leaders who deeply understand this are able to guide their organizations to achieve deep impact and modest profitability.

This harkens to Jim Collins's invaluable monograph, *Good to Great and the Social Sectors*, in which he argued that greatness is at the intersection of what we care deeply about, what we can be best in the world at, and what drives our resource engine.[3] In other words, for nonprofit organizations, being great at something includes being great at resourcing it through direct payment, such as contracts, restricted grants, or fees, or indirect payments by donors inspired to contribute because of a program's relevance and impact. Though times are changing, this idea—this integration of impact and how we resource it—remains a radical one in many parts of our sector. That's why the matrix map process, done thoughtfully and rigorously, is transformative for many leaders. It forces them to acknowledge that mission and resources cannot be separated in any useful or logical manner. Achieving great results requires great resources—time, money, partnerships, and community will—all of which must be intentionally and continuously cultivated.

In fact, this notion of continuous is central to our point of view on sustainability. While the matrix map process of assessing the impact and net financial return of each program in an organization's business model engages an organization's leadership in an intensive inquiry over several months, sustainability is an orientation, not a destination. It is not a one-time thing, not an episodic thing, not a senior management thing or a board of directors thing. It's really a mindset and way of organizational being. The way of thinking about two bottom lines in a holistic way, the sharp financial analysis, and the co-created language around impact all live on well past the creation of the matrix map. When we do this work well, they become inextricably woven into the fabric and culture of the organization.

The Context Today

Nonprofit Sustainability sought to contribute three core ideas to the discourse and practice of nonprofit strategy formation. First, we offered a definition of *sustainability* around which we believe all strategy should be created. Second, we added our voices to a growing choir questioning traditional approaches to nonprofit strategic planning, arguing for much greater emphasis on decision making, execution, and learning. And third, we offered the matrix map tool for analyzing the impact and financial return of a nonprofit's current business model. In the five years that we have been deploying these concepts and tools, the sector-wide discourse about strategy and sustainability has continued to deepen and evolve. We look next at five aspects of that discourse because we think they relate directly to the matrix map process. Leaders and capacity builders who draw on these linkages will be better poised to use our framework effectively.

On Strategy

The momentum of rethinking nonprofit strategy has only grown since we wrote *Nonprofit Sustainability* in 2010. Across all sectors, there is widespread sentiment that traditional strategic planning often does not respond effectively to the strategic questions organizations face now nor to the dynamic external context to which they must adapt and on which they must exert influence. The 2013 article by the

Monitor Institute's O'Donovan and Flower in *The Stanford Social Innovation Review* captures this thinking well and offers a very useful reframe of classic planning activities. The authors contrast classic strategy with the more current adaptive strategy. The former is characterized by "predictions, data collection, and execution from the top down," while the latter is characterized by "experiments, pattern recognition, and execution by the whole."[4] In this definition, the authors speak to a number of concurrent shifts in management and leadership thinking, including "failing fast" through experimentation and "shared leadership" to continuously refine strategies—concepts that deeply influence our thinking about strategy as well. For us, it is not a question of whether to call a given process "strategic planning" but, rather, of ensuring that any process fosters honest analysis and courageous decision making, leading to deeper relevance to our causes and the financial health to resource that relevance over time.

When leaders empower people across the whole organization with the opportunity and responsibility to act strategically in their everyday roles, strategies come to life and get refined as needed in real time.

In *Nonprofit Sustainability*, we expressed this idea that strategy is first and foremost about execution, not predictions (see figure 1.1), which continues to resonate deeply for us and our clients. When leaders empower people across the whole organization with the opportunity and responsibility to act strategically in their everyday roles, strategies come to life and get refined as needed in real time.

On the State of Nonprofit Financial Health

The Nonprofit Finance Fund's 2013 State of the Sector survey results confirmed exactly what we have been experiencing in our strategy and matrix map work with clients across the country: for many organizations, the business models that got them here are not going to get them where they need to go next.[5] Among the findings most salient to the question of strategy formation are these:

+ Forty-two percent of organizations reported that they do not currently have the right mix of financial resources to thrive over the next three years.

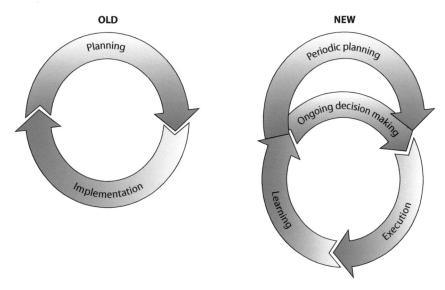

OLD

Planning

Implementation

NEW

Periodic planning

Ongoing decision making

Learning

Execution

Figure 1.1 Nonprofit Strategy: From an Implementation Focus to an Execution and Decision Making Focus

- Thirty-nine percent of organizations plan to change the main ways they raise and spend money in the coming year.
- Fourteen percent of organizations that receive local or state contracts and 17 percent that receive federal contracts are paid full price for the programming they provide.

This degree of economic challenge and business model changes require the kind of adaptive strategy described earlier and the kind of systemwide reckoning with necessary change that the matrix map process engenders.

A second shift in the nonprofit financial health discourse relevant to nonprofit strategy and the matrix map process is the increasing nuance around income diversification. There is growing recognition that each distinct fundraising program requires distinct skills, systems, and leadership. For example, generating meaningful renewable income from an annual event requires different acumen from generating meaningful renewable income from foundation relationships, or from a social enterprise. As thought leader Clara Miller wrote in a 2010 article on the subject, "diversification is subject to the laws of diminishing returns." She further concluded that income diversification shouldn't be labeled a "best practice."[6] Recent work by the consulting firm Bridgespan on how nonprofits scale also points to strategic concentration rather than diversification. Indeed, its research points to three interrelated practices among nonprofits that have scaled. These organizations chose one primary funding stream, ensured that stream was aligned with their mission and approach to the work, and built their professional capacity to manage that funding stream well.[7] We shouldn't conflate changing our core revenue strategy with income diversification, the latter having a connotation of "the more the merrier." There are many groups that need to replace their current primary or secondary revenue stream because it is no longer working for the organization's desired impact or financial health. Most, though, will ultimately be funded by a primary and secondary source, with perhaps three streams at most comprising 95 percent or more of their total income. Revenue strategy is about identifying which revenue streams the organization can win in, not in how many an organization can possibly swim.

We shouldn't conflate changing our core revenue strategy with income diversification, the latter having a connotation of "the more the merrier."

Also in 2013, national research by CompassPoint on the endemic challenges facing nonprofit fundraising elevated the conversation about how many nonprofits are stuck in a vicious cycle of trying to hire their way out of the challenge of raising contributed income rather than embracing the profound and systemwide commitment this kind of fundraising requires. Its report *UnderDeveloped* found pervasive turnover in the development director role and that, moreover, 41 percent of nonprofits with a senior development position on staff nonetheless have no "culture of philanthropy" in their organizations (see the box).[8] In other words, many, many organizations are attempting to raise money from constituents—and no doubt approving annual budgets with associated giving assumptions—without incorporating the core, proven tenets of a successful individual giving program.

DEFINING THE CULTURE OF PHILANTHROPY

Fund development expert and author Simone Joyaux provides this definition:

> Some people define philanthropy as voluntary action for the common good. Many talk about fund development as the engine that drives philanthropy. Without charitable giving, most not-for-profits cannot survive. Philanthropy and fund development—inextricably entwined—belong to the entire organization. Every individual. Every department. All volunteers. This is the culture of philanthropy. An attitude. An understanding. A behavior. After the culture of philanthropy is firmly established, fund development is more effective.[9]

Expert Joan Galon King describes the culture of philanthropy as having these characteristics:

- Everyone behaves as an ambassador, helping to identify new friends and partners.
- The organization operates in a donor-centric fashion, making it easy and comfortable for donors and creating a dialogue.
- Everyone can articulate a case for giving and describe how contributions are used.
- Beneficiaries are viewed as the focus of the organization and invited to share their stories.
- The leadership of the organization is visibly involved in leading fundraising efforts.
- Board members are personally invested and contribute financially.[10]

For us, all of this points to these fundamental questions that nonprofit organizations need to answer:

- What income streams really work for us?
- Which ones are we committed to?
- Which ones will we build and sustain the staffing and systems to thrive in?

Through the matrix map analysis, board and staff are often analyzing together for the first time what it actually costs them to generate income of various types and what the real return on their investment of time, money, and social capital is for each one. This can lead to the strategic abandonment of a vestigial fundraising program or the renewed commitment to invest what it takes to make a funding stream meaningful and renewable over time.

On the Notion of Overhead

Among the most talked about issues since we wrote *Nonprofit Sustainability* has been nonprofit overhead. Dan Pallotta had nearly 3 million views of his TED talk on the subject, with many proclaiming that his message that nonprofits need significant overhead costs to attract talent and deliver high-impact programming transformed their thinking about nonprofit expenditures dramatically.[11] On the other end of the spectrum, Bill Schambra of the Hudson Institute argued that donors have every right to be concerned with overhead and that nonprofits that ignore the natural desire of donors for their dollars to go directly to the issue or constituency that matters to them do so at their peril.[12] Meanwhile, at the federal level, the Office of Management and Budget (OMB) proposed a number of refinements to nonprofit contracting principles, including a significant change to ensure that local and state governments passing through federal dollars to nonprofits in fact cover the full costs of the services they are purchasing.

As we support our clients in the financial analysis necessary to create and interpret their own matrix maps, we always encounter grappling with what constitutes a direct cost and what does not. Frankly, through the lens of achieving exceptional impact in a financially viable way—the core of nonprofit sustainability—debates about overhead ring hollow. The notion that expenses can or should be so neatly categorized is a certain kind of fiction. When a leadership team is assessing where to direct its resources, should it underinvest in program evaluation, storytelling to its constituents, or professional development? Aren't all of these essential to a healthy organization? It is freeing to put aside the complex and often contradictory overhead definitions of a nonprofit's funders, and instead analyze its actual cost to deliver against the actual income generated for each mission-specific and fund development program. This relationship between income and full cost is what every leader needs to know for strategic decision making, regardless of external reporting requirements.

On Impact

The movement and pressure to measure results was well underway when *Nonprofit Sustainability* was published and continues unabated today. The most germane aspect of this discussion to the matrix map process is the question of whether service programs and mainstream organizations contribute to social change. We routinely encounter leadership teams using the matrix map process to challenge themselves on the long-term impact of their programs. We see many fields—from domestic violence, to transitional age youth, to safety net, to arts, to membership organizations of all types—questioning whether their methods for engaging constituents in their programs and in the underlying issues and root causes that make them necessary are as relevant and transformative as they should be.

The Building Movement Project's 2013 monograph series, Advancing Community Level Impact, highlights this growing awareness and energy for change among nonprofit leaders. To engage constituent voices in programming and advocacy, the project encourages what its leaders call "5 percent shifts" in practice— in other words, shifts that don't require wholesale, overnight reinvention.[13] This is deeply aligned with the kind of thinking that the matrix map's impact assessment process fosters. Measuring results is well and good, but the more profound objective is to rethink what we should be measuring in the first place. For many of our strategy clients, that means creating their first-ever theory of change (see the box

Measuring results is well and good, but the more profound objective is to rethink what we should be measuring in the first place.

for a definition). It means leaving behind the hallowed mission statement as the organizing principle for our work, and instead focusing on the strategic selection and design of programs that contribute to a broader change beyond the four walls of the organization.

DEFINING THEORY OF CHANGE

Matthew Forti of Bridgespan defined a theory of change as "an articulation of the results an organization must achieve to be successful, and how it, working alone or with others, will achieve them."[14]

While many definitions abound, an organization's theory of change typically addresses the following questions:

- What is the issue the organization seeks to address?
- What change does the organization anticipate from its actions? We address this more in chapter 4 on articulating intended impact.
- Who is the focus of the organization's desired change?
- What are the primary strategies or interventions that the organization will undertake to either cause or influence the desired change?
- What assumptions about the process or interventions is the organization making?

On Organizational Forms

Perhaps the most existential aspect of the evolving strategy discourse is whether we should be committed to the nonprofit organizational form at all. For some years now, people have talked about sector agnosticism—that young people, for instance, just want to make a difference and don't care which sector they do it in, or that foundations should look for solutions wherever they arise and invest regardless of sector. But more recently, people are questioning the predominant notion that organizations are the primary unit of progressive social change. This is especially prevalent among network and movement strategists. Organizational agnosticism calls for prioritizing the health of a collective or movement as much as, if not more than, the health of each individual nonprofit organization. Management Assistance Group's (MAG) work is emblematic here. In its 2013 report, *Network Leadership Innovation Lab Insights*, the authors identify the structural challenges of being responsible for the sustainability of one's organization—its finances, its board, its staff—and sharing responsibility for the sustainability of the networks and movement of which it is a part.[15] Through this lens, focusing so intently on the sustainability of one's organization through an intensive process like the matrix map could seem like navel gazing or, worse, regressive in some way. In fact, however, rigorous analysis of the relevance and impact of each programmatic endeavor through the matrix map process is essential to reprioritizing how staff and volunteers spend their most precious and expensive resource: time. For leaders to move outside their own organizations to contribute to broader social change, they must first determine what to let go of, how to resource the move, and how to invest in their capacity to thrive in increasingly complex systems.

For leaders to move outside their own organizations to contribute to broader social change, they must first determine what to let go of, how to resource the move, and how to invest in their capacity to thrive in increasingly complex systems

About This Book

The operating environment has never been more complex for nonprofit organizations of all types and the need for our services, programs, and impact more compelling. This complexity, and its corresponding strategic challenges and opportunities, means that staff and board leaders must have a shared and ongoing analysis of their organization's performance on the dual bottom lines of impact and financial health. We have written this second guide to using the matrix map to facilitate that analysis and the strategic decision making of leaders on the front lines of healthy communities and social change.

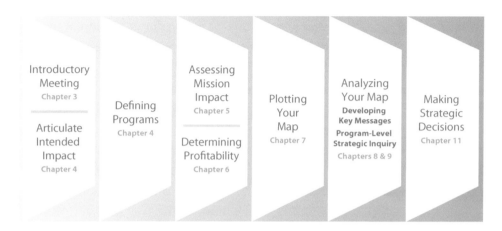

Figure 1.2 The Matrix Map Process

This book is intended as a field guide, inclusive of directions on implementing the matrix map and examples and perspectives from our five years of consulting with the tool. Each chapter is dedicated to an element of matrix map development and analysis, and then we conclude with final guidance to you on ensuring a meaningful and strategic effort (figure 1.2).

We have provided sample meeting agendas and templates for key moments in the matrix map process. As with the first book, our intent is that you can use this guide to self-administer the matrix map or, if you are a consultant, to partner with your clients on it. We begin by introducing you to the matrix map.

The Matrix Map

The dual-bottom-line concept, which integrates mission impact and financial viability, has long been a part of nonprofit theory. But despite widespread knowledge of the concept, it remained challenging to visualize and thereby use to inform decision making. This had the unintended consequence of decisions made while looking at only one aspect. Strategic plans often focused predominantly on accomplishing the mission and developing an array of strategies and objectives for the organization to implement. Budgeting processes too focused a spotlight on producing a balanced financial bottom line, with mission impact often taking a reluctant, but perceived necessary, backseat. Executive directors, as the nexus of mission impact and financial viability, were left to hold this dynamic tension by themselves. The matrix map introduced in *Nonprofit Sustainability* changes this dynamic. By finding a relatively easy way to depict how the organization's activities align and interact to produce exceptional impact and financial viability, the map allows board and staff alike to understand the drivers of impact and revenue and make decisions to strategically grow, shrink, or transform the organization, if necessary, in a way that maximizes impact and promotes sustainability.

In this chapter, we introduce the matrix map as well as the process to create one for your own organization. We begin with a discussion about business models and an overview of the map, explore when you should create one and who should be involved, and then lay out the process.

The Nonprofit Business Model

Business models in for-profit companies explain how an organization creates, delivers, and captures value, which in turn generates profits. Nonprofits replace the word *value* with *impact* and *profits* with *investment through giving*. The value that nonprofit organizations create is the impact of their work, which will change society, enrich lives, and create better places to live. For a nonprofit organization to succeed, though, it also needs its impact to inspire people to pay or invest in the organization. Investment can happen from those directly benefiting from the nonprofit through a fee-for-service revenue strategy that charges a constituent as a consumer of services, indirectly through a philanthropic contribution where someone else is paying for the nonprofit's services as a third party to be delivered to constituents, or a hybrid of the two. Second, investment in the nonprofit sector can take the form of liquid monetary investment in the form of cash or of time or property investment through volunteering and in-kind donations. Because of these differences from for-profits, we define a nonprofit business model as stated in the definition in the sidebar.

This definition focuses on impact and financial viability together, as it is the impact that drives the resources, both financial and nonfinancial, for the organization. Impossible to separate, the impact and finances together make up the business model of a nonprofit and its dual bottom line.

Similar to how the business model definition highlights this integration, every activity in a nonprofit organization contributes to the dual bottom line with its own impact strategy and revenue strategy. Some programs may have fee-for-service or government contracts as their revenue strategy, while others may rely on restricted foundation grants or the generosity of individuals. People often refer, correctly, to these individual revenue strategies as business models. Most nonprofit organizations, however, rely on multiple revenue strategies to create a financially viable enterprise. In our approach, we use the term *business model* to refer to the collective revenue and impact drivers for the overall organization. In doing so, we can make

Definition

Business Model: Leadership's hypothesis about which impacts will engage human and financial participation.

decisions with a sustainability mindset by looking collectively at how the individual programs, each potentially with its own impact and revenue strategy, interact to create a cohesive business model.

Every decision the senior management and board of directors at a nonprofit makes, from the big to the small, affects both the impact and the finances of the organization. Although these aspects are deeply integrated, they are seldom discussed in this manner. Integrating mission impact and financial viability is harder than it sounds. Many traditional systems and structures are not set up that way. For example, a well-put-together financial statement will let you know your operating reserves and whether you're generating a surplus or deficit, but it doesn't let you know the impact of that investment in your program. In the same way, program evaluation reports tell you about impact but don't typically analyze revenue streams, costs, or efficiency information. We tend to look at our organizations through only one lens at a time. However, rather than looking at each of these components separately, we need to assess them together in an integrated manner and make decisions understanding the implications to both our financial viability and mission impact. Only then will we be able to strengthen our organization's business model and pursue sustainability. With the matrix map, we seek to change this perspective.

The Matrix Map

The matrix map, a visual representation of an organization's business model, demonstrates how mission-specific programs and fund development programs work together to create impact and financial viability, thereby reflecting the organization's dual bottom line (figure 2.1). At its most basic, the tool is a two–by-two grid that plots each of the organization's programs or activities by these components.

Each mission-specific program and fund development program is plotted on the axis according to its rating, with mission impact on the vertical axis and

High Mission Impact
Low Profitability

High Mission Impact
High Profitability

Impact →

Profitability →

Low Mission Impact
Low Profitability

Low Mission Impact
High Profitability

Figure 2.1 The Matrix Map

Note: The icons in each quadrant are used in the analysis of the map and are explained in detail in chapter 9.

profitability on the horizontal axis. Breakeven is in the middle of the horizontal axis, showing programs that generate a surplus to the right and those that don't currently or cannot generate a surplus on the left.

The resulting picture presents a unified image allowing board and staff to understand the interaction of the programs with each other and the organization overall rather than looking at each program individually. Taken together it represents the organization's business model, demonstrating the impact of each program or activity of the organization and the outcome of revenue generation and investment. This allows the board and staff to make strategic decisions by understanding the implications of each decision along multiple dimensions and strengthen the business model in the pursuit of sustainability.

Figure 2.2 represents a matrix map for a social service organization, Calhoun Community Center (CCC). We can learn a lot about the organization from looking at this map. For example, we know that it has seven programs: four considered mission-specific programs (after-school tutoring, summer camps, a recreation league, and a community festival) and three fund development programs (individual appeals, foundation grants, and corporate sponsorship). The lighter shade circles represent the fund development programs while the darker shades reflect the mission-specific programs. Each program is placed in the corresponding quadrant on the matrix map based on its assessed impact and determined financial profitability. The size of each circle in this example

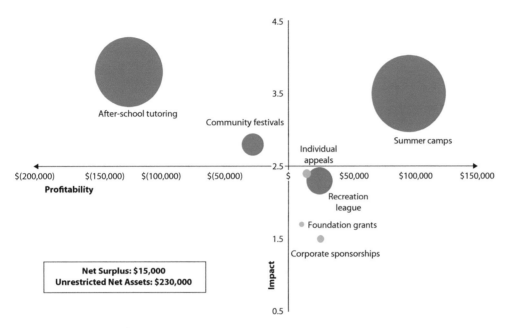

Figure 2.2 Sample Matrix Map

represents the gross expenses of the programs, meaning that summer camps and after-school tutoring are the largest programs of the community center.

The matrix map also tells us about the individual programs, both mission specific and those related to fund development. For example, we know from CCC's map in figure 2.2 that summer camp is a high-impact program that generates a surplus and tutoring is a high-impact program that does not generate sufficient revenue to cover its entire cost. The recreation league, individual appeals, foundation grants, and sponsorships also all generate a surplus.

The map also shows how the programs interact. Collectively the programs work together to generate a modest profit of $15,000. While not done on a one-to-one basis, the surpluses generated by the fund development programs help cover the costs of mission-specific programs including after-school tutoring and the community festival. Similarly, the recreation league, a lower-impact program, generates a surplus that is used to support the organization's finances. Table 2.1 summarizes what the matrix map highlights for an organization.

Often in conversations around annual budgeting, as CCC board and staff struggle to bring the budget into balance, the question is raised, "Why do we offer after-school tutoring? We'd be in a lot better financial shape if we closed that program." Although this is a true statement, it looks only at one bottom line, financial viability, as opposed to the dual bottom line of impact and viability. We can see from the matrix map that after-school tutoring is a high-impact program. A deeper analysis (which we discuss later in the book) would show that no other local organization is providing after-school tutoring and the volunteers for this program drive other aspects of the organization. Instead, the correct question to consider is, "What revenue strategy can we be excellent at to allow us to maintain our after-school tutoring?" or, "Given the amount of revenue we generate, how much can we afford to lose on after-school tutoring?" These are more subjective and strategic question for the board to ponder.

The matrix map helps to frame these important questions for the board and staff to consider in analyzing the financial aspects and mission impact of the organization together. Often as we look at a completed matrix map, the executive director or chief financial officer might think it doesn't necessarily provide any new information. It is in fact true that there is little on the matrix map an informed stakeholder couldn't learn from reading a well-prepared financial statement organized by program or cost center and a good program evaluation. However, not everyone is equally familiar with how to read financial statements (even those who have board training) and not everyone may understand the impact of the programs. The matrix map combines these data in an easy-to-understand way and can engage an entire management team and board in the discussion. Allowing everyone to have the same information and offering a perspective on how best to strengthen

Table 2.1 What the Matrix Map Shows

What the Matrix Map Shows	How It Shows This
What the organization does	Each bubble represents a different program of the organization. Both mission-specific and fund development programs are reflected on the map.
Profitability of each activity	Profitability is measured along the horizontal axis, with the vertical axis crossing at breakeven. The placement of the bubble along this axis shows the profitability of the program. Placement on the right signifies the program generates a surplus, while placement on the left indicates the program isn't able to cover its full costs.
Profitability of the organization	A box explicitly states the financial bottom line reflected in the organization's map.
Relative mission impact of each activity	The vertical axis represents the blended mission impact assessment for each program. Higher placement reflects greater assessed impact of that activity in both absolute terms and relative to other programs. To understand the impact better requires analyzing the criteria used for assessing impact and the scoring the program received.
Where the organization is investing its resources	The circle size represents the gross expenses of each program, allowing us to easily see where the organization is investing the majority of its resources.
Program mix between programming and fund development	The color or shading of the circle identifies the primary purpose of the program: a mission-specific program or a fund development program.
Business model and sustainability	The overall picture reflects how the organization's programs work together to create both impact and financial viability.
How to strengthen the business model	Strategic inquiries provide direction on strategy discussions and decisions necessary to strengthen the overall model.

the organization can lead to a rich discussion that surfaces new ideas and strategies that can be implemented in a sustainable manner.

When Is the Best Time to Put a Matrix Map Together?

Strategic issues arise on their own time line, with new opportunities or lost funding appearing regardless of where the organization is in its strategy cycle. However, for too many organizations, strategic planning is a rote practice done every three to five years. The matrix map is the perfect tool for engaging in strategic discussions at any time and understanding the options and implications in a time-efficient manner.

When an opportunity or a challenge arises, we each tend to focus on one aspect of it, depending on our perspective. If we lose a large contract, the program staff might think about the resulting impact to their programs or overall impact on the organization. Finance staff might immediately think about the lost contribution to overhead and the organization's financial viability. Both are right, but to make a strategic decision moving forward requires integrating these perspectives.

The integration of mission impact and financial viability is often seen when large decisions are being made in an organization, for example, "Should we start a new program?" or, "Should we buy a building?" Of course, at these moments there will be questions and analysis around both finances and impact.

But these components affect every decision, big and small, that senior leadership and the board of directors make. For example when CCC in figure 2.2 is addressing how many hours to offer its tutoring program, it is making both an impact decision—more hours means a deeper level of tutoring for the kids or perhaps more kids served—and a financial decision—more hours means increased costs of staffing and occupancy expenses. Answering questions in isolation makes it hard to understand the implications of the decision on the organization as a whole. Using the matrix map, we can take into consideration the whole organization and make a smart decision.

Outside of emerging challenges and opportunities, many organizations are also proactive about putting matrix maps together, integrating the tool with their periodic and annual planning. The map by itself is a strategic process that drives decision making, impact, and financial viability for an organization. As we'll discuss in chapter 11, some organizations use the matrix map as a core element in setting their organizational strategy; taken together with the intended impact and core strategies and values of an organization, it will make up their cyclical strategic planning process. Others update the map annually as part of the budgeting process so that they always have a current version to use in analyzing and framing discussion throughout the year. The matrix map offers a bridge between strategic planning and operational planning, tying overarching goals for the organization into its daily activities.

Some of the most common times to put together a matrix map are provided in table 2.2.

Table 2.2 When to Put Together a Matrix Map

- Strategic planning process
- Annual budgeting and operational planning
- Loss of funding (to understand implications for the organization)
- New opportunity or funding emerges
- Change in external environment (to understand vulnerabilities)

Here are some key questions to ask in determining if the time is right to put together a matrix map for your organization:

- Are there differing opinions on your board and among your staff as to the role each program plays in your organization?
- Do board members and senior managers sometimes have difficulty looking beyond their favorite programs or areas of responsibility and seeing the organization as a whole?

+ Is your business model under pressure from outside forces?
+ Do you have a decision that needs to be made?

If the answer to any of the questions is yes, the matrix map is the right tool for you to engage everyone in the decision-making process.

Updating the Matrix Map

Regardless of when you put a matrix map together, the question also arises of how often you should update it or create a new map. Some organizations use their matrix map from time to time as a way of monitoring progress, confirming their intuition about how the organization's activities work together and making sure that the leaders and staff are making decisions in an integrated fashion. Others, by virtue of having gone through the exercise once, will keep both impact and finances in mind when making decisions in the future and won't have a need to visualize the business model.

Although there are many times that an organization can put together the matrix map, it isn't meant to be another tool or checkmark that organizations need to complete in order to be "well led." We believe quite the opposite. The matrix map process is designed so that it can be done quickly as well as in a more in-depth manner, but it still takes an organization's most precious resource: time. It is appropriate to ask, "Do we really need the matrix map to understand how our programs work together and make the right decision?"

One word of caution, however: just because the executive director understands how the activities work together does not mean that the rest of the senior leadership team or board of directors, who may not be involved with the activities on a day-to-day basis, understand their interaction. The matrix map is a valuable tool in bringing everyone together in understanding their organization in a new way and making strong decisions about how best to strengthen it.

The matrix map is a valuable tool in bringing everyone together in understanding their organization in a new way and making strong decisions about how best to strengthen it.

Who Should Be Involved in the Matrix Map Process?

Just as there are many options of when to do a matrix map, there are many possible combinations of who should participate in the process. Again, the process is designed such that it can be carried out as quickly as needed or be expansive and inclusive. Regardless of the approach, every key stakeholder can benefit from the matrix map process, and each brings pros and cons in their engagement (table 2.3).

Senior Leadership

Senior leadership engagement in the matrix map process is invaluable. These leaders have a unique perspective on the many facets that make up the organization. They understand the strengths and weaknesses of the mission-specific and fund development programs in deep ways that may not be easily understood even by the board of directors. They also possess an understanding of the organization's niche in the community, have an awareness of the competitive pressures the organization faces, and are familiar with the needs of their constituents. Capturing this knowledge is essential for the matrix map process, especially when assessing the mission impact of each program.

Involving senior leadership can also benefit the organization beyond the matrix map process. Senior leaders often get stuck inside their specific programs, with little time to look around and understand how their colleagues' efforts contribute to the greater whole of the organization. The matrix map is an excellent professional development opportunity to share leadership and engage the professionals leading the organization in seeing the holistic, strategic picture.

Finally, senior leadership involvement is essential when it comes to implementing the strategies designed to strengthen the business model. Sometimes the strategic issues and opportunities identified will be internal or operational. Since it will fall to senior leadership to guide the implementation of any resulting decisions,

Senior leaders often get stuck inside their specific programs, with little time to look around and understand how their colleagues' efforts contribute to the greater whole of the organization.

Table 2.3 Stakeholders to Involve in the Matrix Map

Role	Strengths	Limitations	How to Engage
Senior leadership	In-depth understanding of programs Key role in implementation Professional development opportunity	Internally focused May not know enough about all programs Possible bias toward their own program	As member on task force As team to assess mission impact
Board	Outside perspective that reflects the community Important development opportunity for them to understand the organization at an in-depth level Typically approve the strategic direction	Not enough knowledge to complete the entire mission impact assessment Time commitment	Serve on task force Full board in analyzing the map Potentially in mission impact assessment
Staff	In-depth understanding of their program Opportunity to see the organization in a new way	May not have an in-depth understanding of all programs (depending on the size of the organization) Might feel judged by placement of their own program on the matrix map	Developing detailed information on their program Rollout and explanation of the map prior to implementation of strategic direction
Funders	External and comparative perspective on the organization's programs	In-depth involvement that could limit candor in conversations about impact	Possible survey, perspective to be incorporated in data for mission impact assessment Rollout of matrix map to engage them in better understanding the organization
Constituents	Firsthand knowledge of programs	Directly affected by strategic decisions and profitability of programs	Constituent surveys and data used to inform those taking the mission impact assessment

engaging them early in the process will increase their understanding and also allow them the flexibility to make decisions as they learn from implementation.

Occasionally we've heard the concern that senior leadership will advocate too strongly for their specific program and not be inclined to think of the organization as a whole. This thinking unfairly discounts the passion for the mission that nonprofit professionals feel above and beyond their particular role. Having senior leadership involved in the process as an equal partner with the board of directors will produce the strongest matrix map and analysis possible.

Having senior leadership involved in the process as an equal partner with the board of directors will produce the strongest matrix map and analysis possible.

Board of Directors

Most board members join an organization's board because they believe in the overall mission of the organization or because they have a favorite program that they've been involved with for many years. They often lack an in-depth understanding of the organization's programs, however. The result is that while board members believe in the organization, getting them to understand its inner workings and a complex array of programs is a persistent challenge for executive directors. The matrix map is a useful tool for bringing board members along in the process.

The challenge with boards of directors is engaging them in the appropriate way. Although it can be useful to engage the entire board in the entire process, the members often don't have sufficient information to assess the mission impact of individual programs. Involving the full board in the matrix map process presents an opportunity to educate the board, but it can also add substantial time to the process.

Working with the full board of directors is best when the board consists of a small, engaged group that truly understands the organization's activities. For larger boards, having a couple of representatives serve on a task force responsible for overseeing the process and creating the matrix map is an effective solution. The representatives could include the board chair, treasurer, program committee chair,

The task force is an excellent opportunity for board development of upcoming leaders to learn more about the organization and develop a relationship with the senior leadership.

or development committee chair. The task force is an excellent opportunity for board development of upcoming leaders to learn more about the organization and develop a relationship with the senior leadership.

That doesn't mean there isn't a role for the full board as well. The board of directors is the primary client of the process: they will use the completed matrix map and the resulting analysis in approving the strategic direction for the organization moving forward. The resulting map can engage them in the organization in ways that financial statements and program reports cannot and allow all members to participate in the discussion around the organization's sustainability.

Staff

Beyond senior leadership, the staff's role in the matrix map process may be more in helping them understand the organization in a new way rather than in creating the map. However, some organizations have found it useful to engage staff in the process of assessing mission impact through surveys. This can be helpful provided staff have enough knowledge to accurately and candidly assess the impact of both the mission-specific and fund development programs relative to other programs in the organization and the competitive landscape in the community. We address this step more in chapter 5, but it is important to consider when deciding whom to engage in the process.

Staff involvement typically centers on using the matrix map to develop their skills and understand the organization along the dual bottom line. Sharing the completed map is an excellent opportunity to boost financial literacy among staff by explaining the concepts involved in profitability and engaging them in integrated thinking with impact and finances.

When engaging staff, leadership needs to pay careful attention to how the information is shared and keep focusing on the whole organization and the role that each program plays within the organization as opposed to individual programs. One of the challenges we've seen during the process has been when staff members have resented that "their program" had a lower impact than another or felt that a fund development program was "unimportant" because it didn't have impact. These thoughts are not only untrue in the context of the dual bottom line but destructive to the organization. Leadership needs to educate staff on the multiple roles of programs without prioritizing one over the other or casting judgment. They should also help facilitate a candid conversation while being respectful.

Outside Stakeholders

For the matrix map to be successful and truly useful, it must be built on a candid and open conversation. Sometimes the desire to be inclusive and engage outside stakeholders in the process can inhibit the candor necessary for success. Nevertheless, reaching out to stakeholders such as constituents or funders and using their feedback to inform the mission impact assessment of programs can be very helpful. Surveys of donors who attended an event or customer satisfaction survey of constituents from a program helps inform those charged with creating the matrix map. In addition, foundation representatives can offer perspective on the market of nonprofits in the community that would be useful in assessing impact. Keep in mind that each of these opportunities, while helpful, lengthens the time necessary to complete the process.

Steps in the Process

As you think about which stakeholders to engage in the process, it may be helpful to know more about the steps. Depending on when your organization chooses to put together a matrix map, you may want a quick process or a more thorough one. For example, if you have been offered a grant opportunity to start a new

Figure 2.3 The Matrix Map Process

mission-specific program, you may want to create a matrix map quickly to see how it would fit in with your organization's other programs. If the goal is to build board and staff understanding of the organization's business model, a longer process is useful. In this book, we present a longer version of the process but also note in "The Quicker Map" sections when things can be condensed.

The steps in the process are as follows (figure 2.3):

* *Introduce the process.* The goal of the introductory meeting is to ensure that everyone in the process understands the concept of the dual bottom line, the matrix map, and the process for putting it together. It is also the time to identify the strategic issues the organization is addressing through this process. Chapter 3 covers the introductory meeting.
* *Articulate the intended impact.* For many organizations, the impact that the organization strives for goes unarticulated since it is assumed that everyone understands the intentions. Clarifying and focusing the desired outcome of the efforts is an important first step in then matrix map process.

- *Define the programs.* The matrix map reflects both the mission-specific and fund development programs of an organization. Choosing them may seem like a straightforward, easy step, but if you don't choose the right ones, the resulting map will tell you no more than you already knew. Chapter 4 covers both articulating your intended impact and the process for choosing the programs to map.

- *Assess the impact.* In our matrix map process, we used a blended impact assessment that takes into account core competencies, competitive pressures, and contribution to the intended impact. It is an opportunity for an open discussion and crucial to the success of this process. Chapter 5 walks you through the process for assessing the impact of your programs.

- *Determine profitability.* Surprisingly, even for finance professionals, the concept of determining program profitability may be new. Chapter 6 explains how to do so, including allocating shared and administrative expenses.

- *Plot the map.* Once all of the raw materials (programs, mission impact scores, and profitability data) are in place, you can draw your matrix map by hand or use spreadsheet software like Microsoft Excel to plot the map using an Excel bubble chart. A couple of tricks when using the software will help make your matrix map much more readable. Chapter 7 explains them all.

- *Analyze the map.* The true power of the matrix map comes from analyzing the map and knowing which steps to take to strengthen you business model. Chapter 8 takes a look at the big picture in helping you decipher the message of the map, with chapter 9 focusing on more specific program-level strategy.

- *Make strategic decisions.* The matrix map can help staff and board better understand your organization's business model, but the only way to strengthen it is to actually make strategic decisions. Our goal is that this book and process will lead you and your board to this step.

The power of these steps lies in their ability to transform your organization and increase your sustainability.

Summary: Using this Field Guide

The first part of the matrix map process is to create a coherent, integrated, and meaningful image of the organization's business model. This includes defining programs to map, gathering information to assess mission impact, determining profitability, and physically creating the map. We then turn to analyzing and strengthening the business model by understanding the strategic questions, brainstorming impact and revenue strategies, and making strategic decisions. As we mentioned above, each step in the process can expand or contract depending on the time available. The expanded version allows an increased understanding of the organization's programs as well as professional development of staff as they share experiences with each other, which is immensely helpful in implementation and future strategic discussions. An expedited process in "The Quicker Map" provides you with information to make immediate decisions that integrate impact and financial strategy.

Throughout the book, you'll find examples of how the process is implemented, and we've provided templates for you to do the same on your own. These templates can also be found online at www.nonprofitsustainability.org.

Let's get started.

Getting Started

When you throw a party, you start by deciding on your guest list. The process of creating a matrix map to visualize and strengthen your business model is very similar. To begin the process, we examine who to invite to be on the task force guiding the process. This chapter also sets the agenda for the introductory meeting, which makes sure participants understand the fundamental principles of the matrix map and establishes the structure of the map by identifying the strategic issues the organization is grappling with and the mission-specific and fund development programs we want to map (figure 3.1).

Figure 3.1 The Matrix Map Process: Introductory Meeting

Guiding the Process: Establishing a Task Force

Success in setting and implementing strategy starts by creating a group of people tasked with guiding the process. Establishing a task force to oversee both the creation and analysis of the matrix map allows a group within the organization to be part of the map process, which creates an understanding of the dual bottom line of your organization and the steps for strengthening it. This opportunity also develops key stakeholders, whether they are board members or staff, and leads to a greater likelihood that any changes resulting from the matrix map process will be embraced and implemented.

Template 3.1 provides an action guide for managing your task force. The responsibilities outlined in the template can be used as a description of the task force responsibilities when recruiting members. These are the key responsibilities:

- Understand the principles behind the matrix map to guide an effective process in creating one for the organization.
- Identify the strategic issues facing the organization and articulate the organization's intended impact. Then determine programs to map in a manner that reflects the intended impact and captures the strategic issues.
- Determine the criteria and methodology to assess the mission impact of all mission-specific and fund development programs and implement the process.
- Gather background data on mission-specific and fund development programs to inform the impact assessment.
- Working with the finance department, calculate the profitability of all programs.
- Collect all data and create the matrix map.
- Provide analysis based on the matrix map framework and facilitate discussions with senior management and the board resulting in strategic decision making.
- Work with senior management to present the matrix map, its concepts and analysis, to the organization's entire staff.

TEMPLATE 3.1   TASK FORCE ACTION GUIDE

Description	Who Is Needed	Time Line	End Date
Understand the principles behind the matrix map to guide an effective process in creating a map for the organization.			
Identify the strategic issues facing the organization.			
Articulate the intended impact.			
Identify mission-specific and fund development programs			
Define and tailor the mission impact criteria.			
Determine the methodology for assessing impact—in person or through an e-survey.			
Gather background data on mission-specific and fund development programs.			
Determine the profitability of existing programs.			
Assess the initial mission impact, discuss results, and finalize the mission impact assessment.			
Create the matrix map.			
Analyze the matrix map with strategic inquiries and facilitate initial discussions.			
Present the matrix map to the board for strategic decision making.			
Present the matrix map to the staff.			

Template 3.1, which can be completed at the introductory meeting, provides an action guide for the task force with a complete list of tasks to move the process forward.

The task force is responsible not only for overseeing the matrix map process, but also for making meaning of the resulting picture. The task force works with the board of directors and staff to help them understand the matrix map and explain any significant changes to the organization's programmatic makeup.

With the success of the matrix map process in the hands of the task force, it is important to select the right people and the right number of people. Too large a group becomes unwieldy: you'll spend most of your time trying to coordinate schedules for meetings. Too small a group will invite valid complaints that the process was too insular and could bog down the analysis with the question of whether the right people were in the room for the assessment. Although there is no hard rule, task forces typically should be no more than eight people, with six to eight usually an ideal number.

More important than the number, the question of who is on the task force is essential. In chapter 2, we discussed the relative merits of each stakeholder's participation. A task force that comprises the senior management team positions itself well to have an in-depth understanding of the organization's strategic issues, programs, and operating environment. It also offers staff an opportunity to learn more, test their assumptions about other programs, and look at the organization as an entire system. Program managers often are so deeply immersed within their own program they may not have an opportunity to see how it relates to the entire organization in a systematic manner. Allowing them to explore this context through the matrix map creates stronger leaders and can influence their day-to-day management. These leaders will be responsible for implementing any strategic decisions that come out of the process, and participating on the task force gives them a thorough understanding of the matrix map and informs their ongoing decision making.

A task force that comprises the senior management team also offers staff an opportunity to learn more, test their assumptions about other programs, and look at the organization as an entire system.

Beyond nonprofit staff, board member engagement on the task force is also helpful. The board will typically be more fully involved in the analysis and decision-making components of the process, but having one or two board members who have deep knowledge of the organization's programs or fundraising is helpful.

The time commitment for the task force does not need to be overwhelming. In our process, the task force meets three to four times for a couple of hours at a time.

Choosing a Project Manager

The matrix map process has a number of components, with multiple pieces of information that need to be collected, summarized, and communicated to several stakeholders. Assign someone on the task force to serve as the project manager for the process. We recommend this even if you've engaged an outside consultant. This is an excellent professional development opportunity for a staff person who is interested and you want to engage in the process. The project manager is responsible for managing documents, coordinating and facilitating meetings of the task force, creating the mission impact survey and any other documents that may be needed, and generally moving the process along the time line.

Introductory Meeting

Once the task force participants are determined, an introductory meeting designed to provide an overview of the matrix map concept and to surface strategic issues will help the group get started on the right foot. At the conclusion of the meeting, the members can complete the action guide in template 3.1 to assign responsibility for specific steps and move the process along. Template 3.2 sets out an agenda for this introductory meeting.

Schedule enough time for the introductory meeting. Two hours should be sufficient. You'll be happy that you spent this time at the start to make sure everyone

Tip

The Quicker Map

If you know the strategic questions you're trying to answer, make sure you form the task force with the right people and decision makers at the table. If this is primarily an operational issue, it may not be necessary to have board participation, which can make scheduling meetings easier.

understands the process and theory of the matrix map and to make sure that your map is structured correctly. Let's take a look at the agenda:

- *Introductions:* Depending on the makeup of your task force, members may know each other very well. If, however, you have board members on your task force, take a moment for them to get to know the staff and for staff to learn a little bit about them.
- *Overview of the concept:* Before diving in to the work of putting together a matrix map, make sure everyone understands the concept. Review the integration of mission impact and financial viability in nonprofit business models and the matrix map. For some members of the task force, the concepts may seem like second nature, but not everyone in the room may be as familiar

---

TEMPLATE 3.2   INTRODUCTORY MEETING AGENDA

Goals

- Understand the matrix map and the process.
- Assign roles and determine time lines.
- Articulate strategic issues facing the organization.

Agenda

- Introductions
- Matrix map overview
- Review and completion of the task force action guide (template 3.1)
- Strategic issues
- Next meeting

with them. Having everyone understand the concepts at the beginning will help the analysis later.

+ *Completion of the action guide:* Assign responsibility for specific tasks for the matrix map. This will also provide an opportunity to discuss the time commitment required for the task force and the matrix map process overall to make sure it fits within everyone's schedule.

+ *Identifying strategic issues:* Any planning process works best when you've identified the strategic issues that your organization is facing. For the matrix map, having a sense of the issues will guide the task force in structuring the map to best address them.

Coming out of the introductory meeting, the task force will have an understanding of the matrix map, the process for creating one, their roles and time line for doing so, and the strategic issues your organization is facing.

Overview of the Concept

To begin the process, it is important that everyone understands the interconnectedness between mission impact and financial viability that we noted in chapter 2.

This discussion should begin with the business model. Nonprofit business models are different from for-profit business models in that they encompass both finances and impact. We already defined the business model as leadership's hypothesis about which impacts will engage human and financial participation. The definition builds on the impact as the value proposition of the organization. It also recognizes that resource development for nonprofits may be both financial as well as volunteer hours and in-kind donations.

Beyond the definition of business model, it is important for the task force to understand the nature of business models. First, business models change over time. Sustainability is an orientation, not a destination. What is sustainable today may or may not be sustainable into the future. This is common and important, because sometimes senior staff can feel that they chose the "wrong" business model. Rather, business models evolve. We're currently seeing historic shifts in nonprofit business models as organizations that are primarily government funded see cuts to their services and are searching for other business models. It does not mean that this was a poor business model, just that it may not be the right business model moving forward.

Second, business models are unique. Often people enter this process thinking that there is one "right" business model for their organization, and if they can just find that model and import it as their own, all of their problems will be solved. Unfortunately, that is not how it works. All of us live in different communities with different strengths and different funding structures. What might work in one community wouldn't necessarily work in another. Organizations can have very similar missions but different business models. For example, a college prep nonprofit in an upper-middle-class area might charge a fee for service, while a similar organization serving at-risk youth would rely on foundation and corporate support. Both of these are business models that work for those organizations.

As organizations begin the matrix map process, they are not looking externally for the right answer but rather looking internally to understand their own strengths and how they interact with the external environment and then figuring out how to leverage them into a sustainable model.

Introducing the Matrix Map

Beyond the business model, now is also the time to introduce participants to the matrix map. Building on the concepts of the dual bottom line of mission and money, show how the grid plots an organization's activities based on their mission impact and financial profitability. Having a sample matrix map to share with participants so they know what they're working toward is helpful. (You can use a sample from one of our case studies in chapter 10 if you wish.)

The purpose of this introduction is to put participants in the right frame of mind and help them understand where the organization is going. Now is the time to start thinking about your organization's strategic issues.

Identifying Strategic Issues

Staff and board members may feel that they know the strategic issues facing the organization, but they're rarely articulated in one central place. As we start the process, we want to be intentional about calling out the strategic challenges your organization faces and make sure there is agreement among the task force members. Strategic issues are likely to come from any number of sources: constituent needs, funding trends, other external forces such as the market landscape and political landscape, and other internal forces including human resources (staff, volunteers and the board), culture, and infrastructure.

These are highlighted in figure 3.2. Template 3.3 summarizes the pressures and provides questions for discussion that can be used to surface issues and then prioritize among them.

Constituent Needs

Understanding and addressing the needs of constituents is at the heart of impact for many nonprofit organizations. Even outside of social services, understanding your constituents and how you relate with them is essential. In identifying strategic issues in this

Tip

The Quicker Map

If you've created a matrix map previously, your staff members are probably already steeped in the methodology. You can bypass this part of the process.

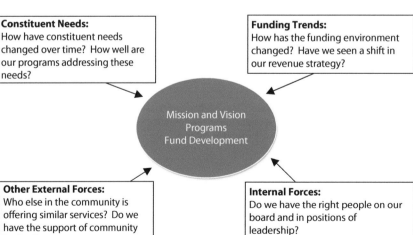

Constituent Needs: How have constituent needs changed over time? How well are our programs addressing these needs?

Funding Trends: How has the funding environment changed? Have we seen a shift in our revenue strategy?

Other External Forces: Who else in the community is offering similar services? Do we have the support of community leaders?

Internal Forces: Do we have the right people on our board and in positions of leadership?

Mission and Vision
Programs
Fund Development

Figure 3.2 Strategic Pressures

TEMPLATE 3.3   IDENTIFYING STRATEGIC ISSUES

Use the questions that follow to surface and discuss strategic issues. Capture your thoughts under each category. Then summarize and prioritize your top strategic issues.

Constituent Needs	Funding Trends
What are the top three needs our constituents have today?	What is the percentage of earned revenue versus philanthropic support our organization receives, and how has this changed over the past three years?
Do immediate and long-term needs differ? If so, how?	What are the main revenue streams for the organization, what percentage of revenue are they for the organization, and how have those changed in the past three years?
How have these needs evolved over the past five years?	What is the organization's operating reserves, and how have they changed over the past three years?
How well do our programs directly address these needs?	Do we know the surplus generated or subsidy required for each business line? Have these changed significantly over the past three years?
How has demand for our services changed over the past three years?	How has the funding environment changed over the past three years? Do we see this continuing?
How has the evaluation of our programs been over the past three years?	

Other External Forces	Internal Forces
Who else in the community is offering similar services to ours? Do we have a competitive or collaborative relationship with them?	Have we had significant turnover in the past two years?
Is there a larger movement or network of organizations working toward a similar impact as our organization?	
Are for-profit companies entering our service space?	Do we have the right personnel with the right qualifications and attitude in the right positions?
Are community leaders, elected and others, supportive of our organization's mission, or is there is a divide in support?	Does our organization have a culture of excellence?

Have we received negative press in the past two years? If so, has this affected the perception of potential funders? Write your thoughts below:	How well does our board understand the organization's business model, and how engaged are they in strategic decisions? Does leadership have the accurate and timely information they need to govern and lead the organization?
Constituent Needs	**Funding Trends**
Other External Forces	**Internal Forces**

area, the goal is to understand your constituents and whether you are aligned with them. Some key questions to ask are:

+ What are the top three needs our constituents have today?
+ Do immediate and long-term needs differ? If so, how?
+ How have these needs evolved over the past five years?
+ How well do our programs directly address these needs?
+ How has demand for our services changed over the past three years?
+ How has the evaluation of our programs been over the last three years?

Funding Trends

Almost all nonprofits face funding pressure at some point during their fiscal year. As you think about funding trends in terms of strategic issues, look beyond day-to-day operations to understand bigger trends that may be straining your financial structure. Consider these questions in specifying strategic issues:

+ What is the percentage of earned revenue versus philanthropic support our organization receives, and how has this changed over the past three years?
+ What are the main revenue streams for the organization, what percentage of revenue are they for the organization, and how have those changed in the past three years?
+ What is the organization's operating reserve, and how has it changed over the past three years?
+ Do we know the surplus generated or deficit accumulated for each program? Have these changed significantly over the past three years?
+ How has the funding environment changed over the past three years? Do we see this continuing?

Other External Forces

Whereas constituent needs and funding trends relate to the mission impact and financial viability of the organization, this category of external forces and the next one (internal forces) influence the organization's ability to meet both of those. External forces refer to anything outside the organization that may affect its ability to be sustainable, such as the competitive landscape or political environment. Some key questions to ask when surfacing strategic issues here are:

+ Who else in the community is offering similar services to ours, and do we have a competitive or collaborative relationship with them?
+ Is there a larger movement or network of organizations working toward a similar impact as our organization?

- Are for-profit companies entering our service space?
- Are community leaders, elected and others, supportive of our organization's mission, or is there is a divide in support?
- Have we received negative press in the past two years? If so, has this affected the perception of potential funders?

Internal Forces

Internal forces are those influences within an organization that may adversely affect an organization's sustainability. Human capital, that is, having the right people on staff or as volunteers, is a significant internal force, as is having the right board members for the organization. Leadership transition or succession planning is another internal force, along with the culture of an organization. Beyond people, systems, processes, and infrastructure, are there other internal forces that may have an impact on your organization's ability to thrive? Some questions to ask in surfacing strategic issues include:

- Have we had significant turnover in the past two years?
- Do we have the right personnel with the right qualifications and attitude in the right positions?
- Does our organization have a culture of excellence?
- How well does our board understand the organization's business model, and how engaged are the members in strategic decisions?
- Does leadership have the accurate and timely information they need to govern and lead the organization?

Articulating Strategic Issues

The questions about the strategic issues are meant to be a guide to help you think expansively and specifically about the key strategic issues facing your organization.

They are not necessarily meant to be gone through and answered individually. Rather, most senior leaders have an idea of the strategic issues when entering the meeting. These questions are meant to help check your assumptions and make sure your thoughts are comprehensive and complete.

Strategic issues manifest themselves in different ways. Consider these examples:

> "We're running perpetual deficits and have eaten through our reserves. We need to better understand our finances and come up with a more sustainable business model."
>
> "There is a new Request for Proposal that has been issued by the county government for a service that is tangentially related to our mission. Should our organization pursue the contract? If we win, what are the implications on the rest of our organization and business model?"
>
> "We recently learned that our signature program, which has long been supported by the community foundation, will receive a substantially smaller grant in the next fiscal year."

Sometimes strategic issues can be daunting because a solution may not be obvious. This is to be expected and you shouldn't fall into the trap of thinking that you need to know a solution today. Rather, the matrix map framework will help engage the brightest minds within the organization to collectively find a solution. Template 3.3 provides space to capture your thoughts on each of the pressures affecting your organization. After you've discussed them, identify your top strategic issues. Having the issues identified at the beginning of the process will help unite the task force in searching together for the solution.

Tip

The Quicker Map

You may be approaching the matrix map because you already know the strategic issue your organization is facing. If this is the case, you can replace the section of your first meeting from surfacing strategic issues to confirming strategic issues to make sure everyone is in agreement.

Templates

Go to www.nonprofitsustainability.org for online access to the following templates from this chapter:

- Task Force Action Guide: Describes the purpose and duties of the task force to guide the process
- Introductory Meeting Agenda: Sample agenda for the introductory meeting
- Identifying Strategic Issues: Lists the areas to consider when identifying your strategic issues

Summary

All good journeys begin with a first step, and the path toward greater sustainability is no different. This journey begins by putting together a task force to help guide your process, create the matrix map, and analyze the results. The task force typically consists of senior management and board representatives, but the makeup may vary depending on your strategic issues. Start by making sure everyone is aware of the dual-bottom-line concept and the purpose of the matrix map. Then make sure there is a shared agreement about the strategic issues that your organization is facing. At the conclusion of this introductory meeting, there should be awareness of the issues facing the organization and the process for engaging leadership in making strategic decisions to address them.

Articulating Impact

I t was the author Lewis Carroll who wrote, "If you don't know where you're going, any road will get you there." For nonprofit organizations the "where you're going" translates into the impact they hope their efforts will accomplish.

Much has been written in recent years about the shift among nonprofits to a greater focus on impact. From strategic philanthropy among donors and foundations to social impact bonds among government agencies, there is increased interest in the results and outcomes nonprofits produce. Even with these sector-wide conversations, internal discussions about the specific desired impact of an organization and its programs, while more widespread than they used to be, remain rare.

Many organizations use their mission statement to provide direction, but these statements are often broadly written, resulting in little direction to leadership in setting priorities or strategy. For the matrix map to reflect a program's candid and meaningful contribution to an organization's impact, there must first be a shared understanding among board and staff of what the overall organization aims to accomplish. Therefore, even before defining programs and beginning to create a matrix map, the task force lays the foundation by making explicit the organization's intended impact. The second meeting of the task force centers around the next two steps in the matrix map process: articulating the impact and defining the programs to map (figure 4.1).

Figure 4.1 The Matrix Map Process: Articulate Intended Impact and Defining Programs

Understanding Impact

Susan Colby, Nan Stone, and Paul Carttar of Bridgespan defined *intended impact* in a *Stanford Social Innovation Review* article as "a statement or series of statements about what the organization is trying to achieve and will hold itself accountable for within some manageable period of time. It identifies both the benefits the organization seeks to provide and the beneficiaries."[1]

Crafting a strong impact statement is a delicate balance between setting a large "audacious" goal and one that the organization can meaningfully contribute to.

The statement of intended impact serves as a beacon illuminating the primary issue or problem the organization is trying to address by stating the desired outcome it seeks. It is complementary to the mission statement, but is more of an internal statement used to narrow the mission and provide focus around the core outcomes of the organization. Crafting a strong impact statement is a delicate balance between setting a large "audacious" goal and one that the organization can meaningfully contribute to.

While a nonprofit's presence and outcomes may result in numerous positive benefits to the community, the intended impact focuses on the core result of the organization's work, treating the other results as positive by-products of the organization's efforts. For example, an organization that focuses on reducing neighborhood crime may also contribute to an increase in property values and quality of life. However, because so many other factors go into these outcomes, the intended impact of the organization's efforts is crime reduction. No organization completely controls or can take credit for any outcome, but there should be a logical linkage between the organization's programs and the intended impact. In our data-driven world, it may seem ideal for measurements to show the connection, but at the very least, we should be able to know that the programs significantly contribute to the stated impact. Finally, the purpose in creating a statement of intended impact is not to create goals such as, "100% of all children will be able to read at the appropriate grade level by third grade," but rather to know how to monitor progress toward the intended impact.

No organization completely controls or can take credit for any outcome, but there should be a logical linkage between the organization's programs and the intended impact.

As an example, a community-based organization that supports girls in graduating from high school has the mission statement of "lifting up the next generation by supporting women and girls." However, this organization's intended impact statement is much more specific: "Our organization supports women and girls between the ages of 10 and 18 to enable them to graduate high school." The intended impact in this statement more specifically states whom the organization is trying to reach (girls between the ages of 10 and 18) and how it will monitor progress (high school graduation rates). Although there may be many different strategies the organization could adopt to accomplish its impact, the statement sets a target in graduation rates to use in prioritizing and making strategic decisions.

Articulating Intended Impact

One of the key criteria in assessing the mission impact of both the mission-specific and fund development programs is contribution to intended impact. We'll discuss that process in more detail in the next chapter, but in addition to being important for leading your organization, having agreement around the organization's intended impact is critical to developing a meaningful map.

Most stakeholders in an organization already have subconsciously articulated the intended impact. It is typically tied very closely with their beliefs and the reason behind their involvement in the organization. The process to craft the statement is designed to surface these thoughts and articulate the current impact. At this stage in the process, you are not necessarily creating a new impact for the organization, but documenting the current impact in a statement. To do so, survey the matrix map task force to surface thoughts, search for themes, and draft an initial statement.

The following questions are particularly helpful in eliciting initial themes around an organization's impact:

+ *What is the issue or problem the organization is trying to address?* The heart of the impact statement should name the primary issue or problem the organization is trying to address. For example, a low-income housing agency may be fighting the lack of adequate, affordable housing for the city's low-income population, whereas a history museum's issue might be connecting people to their past. Larger, more comprehensive organizations may be trying to address several issues or problems, but the task force should try to focus on the core reason the organization exists. Ultimately the goal is to craft a statement that focuses on this problem.

+ *If we went away today, who would it matter to, and why?* This question focuses on a negative aspect—the organization no longer exists—but is another way of getting at the impact of the organization. Imagining a community without the nonprofit organization helps cut through the clutter and reveals the core of the most important aspects of the organization.

+ *Who are the primary direct beneficiaries of our organization?* For many organizations, the general public is a beneficiary of the organization's important work, but this question seeks to understand who is at the center of that work. An organization may serve many different constituencies, but some may be served in support of a primary beneficiary. In our previous example, teenage girls are the primary beneficiary, but the organization also serves parents, offering them skills to support their daughters. While this is another constituency, the organization's primary beneficiaries are the teen girls.

+ *What is the geographic region of our impact?* Just like constituencies, organizations may expand their geographic footprint over time. This question surfaces whether there is a target neighborhood or community where the organization focuses. This does not necessarily mean the organization would not work in other areas, but it is important to understand the core area at the center of their impact.

+ *What does success look like, and how can it be measured?* Combining this two-part question into one forces the respondent to be specific about the changes caused by the organization. Often measurements are used as metrics in the intended impact statement. Even if you can't come up with metrics, describe the changes as a result of the success of the organization.

These are hard questions to answer, but for many who are involved in and dedicated to an organization's success, they are also implicit in their passion. They answer the question of why an organization carries out its work. Participants in the process should not overthink their responses because their initial response is often the most candid and helpful.

Having the task force answer the questions on their own first allows them an opportunity to think through their responses and then bring them to a meeting for discussion. Sharing the answers to each question and searching for similarities and differences can be an enlightening conversation about the organization's impact. Themes from the responses will emerge and should be written down. After everyone has had a turn to answer all the questions, gather the themes and draft an impact statement.

These can be robust discussions, and we recommend spending at least two hours for this meeting. Sometimes it may be helpful to draft an impact statement, let it percolate for a couple of days, and then revisit it. Inevitably these conversations may lead to larger fundamental questions about the direction of the organization, and it may be worthwhile to pause the process and consult with the entire board on the impact statement before moving forward. Template 4.1 outlines the agenda for the meeting, template 4.2 provides an overview of the concept for distribution to the task force, and template 4.3 provides the survey and sheet to record responses.

TEMPLATE 4.1   TASK FORCE MEETING AGENDA: INTENDED IMPACT AND PROGRAMS

Goals

- Articulate intended impact
- Determine mission-specific and fund development programs to map

Agenda

- Articulate intended impact (for examples, see the "Intended Impact Examples" tip)
- Share responses from survey questions. Go person-by-person and then summarize asking:

  Where are the similarities?

  - Is there a theme?
  - Who are our constituents?
  - What outcome do we seek?
  - Draft a statement

  How do we measure success?

- Determine mission-specific and fund development programs to map

TEMPLATE 4.2   INTENDED IMPACT SURVEY

A statement of intended impact is a specific statement about what the organization will accomplish and for what it will be held accountable. It focuses the organization and defines whom it serves and the desired outcome.

We will begin by asking a series of questions about our organization. There is no right or wrong answer, but please try to be specific. We will discuss the answers at the next task force meeting.

These are the question we'll address for the survey:

- What is the issue or problem we are trying to address?
- If we went away today, who would it matter to, and why?
- Who are the primary direct beneficiaries of our organization?
- What is the geographic region of our impact?
- What does success look like, and how can it be measured?

Tip

The Quicker Map

A statement of intended impact can serve an organization for years. Once you've developed one for your organization, you can reaffirm it in this process and then move on if it is still valid. There is no need to redraft a statement of intended impact unless something substantial has changed within your organization or your community. However, the metrics by which you measure your impact can be changed from time to time as you learn more about how helpful they are.

Although this exercise is typically easier for social service, health care, and education organizations, it can add value for any nonprofit organization. Discussions on impact for arts and culture organizations as well as advocacy organizations and other subsectors are important to establish a shared purpose for the work. In addition, the focus on impact in the nonprofit sector from funding sources is happening across the spectrum of missions; a statement of intended impact can help position an organization for the future.

The intended impact statement is an internal statement and doesn't need to be shared publicly. It may take several drafts to come up with a statement that the task force feels comfortable using. After a draft is written, a candid discussion framed by a statement of intended impact can help differentiate the contribution that programs have toward the organization's intended impact. However, before that, the task force must first identify the programs—both mission-specific programs and fund development programs—that they want to map.

Tip

Intended Impact Examples

Here are some examples of intended impact for organizations:

Early childhood organization: We work with low-income children between the ages of 3 months to 5 years old to enable them to enter first grade healthy and prepared for their education as compared to state standards.

Museum: Through engaging and interactive exhibits, we ignite the minds of youth living in our city and connect them to the broader world.

Youth counseling: Our organization develops a sustainable support structure for youth in crisis under the age of 25 as measured by reconnections with family and evaluation.

TEMPLATE 4.3   INTENDED IMPACT THEMES AND DRAFT

Themes: Issues or Problem Addressed   **Impact Themes**

-

-

Target Constituents   **Geography**   **Impact Measures**

Current Mission Statement

Intended Impact Statement

Defining Programs to Map

At first glance, the thought of defining your organization's programs may seem simple enough: you know which mission-specific programs you run, add in some fund development programs, and you have your list. But when was the last time you thought systematically about what your organization does and how it does it? While it may be easy to overlook this step, if you don't spend some time thinking about how best to structure or group your programs, you might end up with a matrix map that doesn't tell you what you need to know to meet your strategic issue and improve your sustainability.

The organization's programs should represent both the mission-specific programs the organization runs to accomplish its mission and the fund development programs whose primary goal is to generate resources. Many terms have been used to describe these programs. In our previous book, we used *business lines*; others prefer the term *activities*. These terms are interchangeable, and you should use whichever one is more comfortable for your task force and board. However, whichever term you use, make sure you include both mission-specific activities such as direct services and advocacy and fund development activities such as special events or major donor solicitation.

The organization's programs should represent both the mission-specific programs the organization runs to accomplish its mission and the fund development programs whose primary goal is to generate resources.

Mission-Specific Programs

Articulating your mission-specific programs may be as easy as listing the two, three, or more programs that your organization operates. For example, an environmental organization may have water quality testing, community education, and river cleanup programs. As you list the programs, you'll want to see how the strategic issues previously identified are reflected in the programs. Some possible examples of structures are by geographic area served, activity, or funding source. Let's take a closer look at some of the structure options.

Geography versus Activity

Two similar organizations that separately served Colorado and Wyoming merged, creating a large geographic service area. As the new organization began the matrix map process, the strategic issue that emerged was the performance of the satellite offices and whether they needed or could afford each of the offices. The task force decided to map the organization's mission-specific programs by geography, with each office being its own program. They also included fund development programs, which were primarily responsible for generating unrestricted funding. This structure allowed the task force to understand better which offices were creating impact and what investment was required for each office.

After creating the structure, analyzing the map, and making some strategic decisions, the task force turned to another strategic issue: the mix of their programming between research and direct service. Unfortunately, having the map structured by geography didn't help them in better understanding their organization. To answer this question, they prepared a matrix map that was structured around activities. In doing so, they created a map that showcased the impact that each type of mission-specific program was having and the investment required for that impact. This aided in a robust discussion about the right mix of activities for their organizations. Together, the two maps provided a framework for the board and staff to make decisions about what services they would offer and where they would offer them.

We're not advocating here for organizations to make two matrix maps as part of the routine, but rather emphasizing that the structure of a map needs to reflect the strategic issues the organization is facing.

Mapping by Funding Source

Organizations that operate large government contracts often tend to define their programs internally by the funding source. An after-school program becomes "DCYF [Department of Children, Youth and Families] program" or a domestic violence shelter becomes the "HHS [Health and Human Services] program." This is an example of a source-based accounting approach that focuses on the source of funding for an activity as opposed to the activity itself.

Whenever possible, mission-specific programs should be identified by the activity that the organization operates as opposed to the source of funds. In doing so, programs will reflect the activities that an organization undertakes to accomplish its mission and intended impact. Restricted funding sources like government contracts, while crucial, are only a vehicle for funding an organization's efforts. They may increase or decrease over time, but if an activity is essential to an organization's impact, the program should be named after the activity and then the matrix map should be used as a tool to sustain the impact and create financial viability for the organization. This is especially helpful in the analysis of the map when there may be a need to develop strategies to invest in fund development programs to generate significant revenue to support high-impact mission-specific programs that are not fully funded by government agencies or other funding sources.

Again, you should let the strategic issues of your organization help guide the structure of your programs. For example, if your key strategic issue is that you are losing government funding and you want the matrix map to illuminate the potential challenge this presents, it may make sense to have the mission-specific programs organized by funding source. If your issue is more centered around identifying alternative revenue strategies to support your impact, then it makes more sense to have your analysis, discussion, and mission-specific programs center on the core activities of the organization rather than funding sources.

Keeping your mind open to all these and other possible structures, revisit the strategic issues that you listed previously. As you make an initial draft of your programs, check to see that they are reflected in either the mission-specific or fund development programs you've chosen.

Fund Development Programs

Defining mission-specific programs may seem comfortable for the task force, but they may not be as used to doing so with fund development programs. For purposes of the matrix map, we separate out fund development programs to reflect the activities that drive unrestricted funding. It is tempting for organizations to combine these into one fundraising program, but avoid this temptation. Every fundraising activity has a different return on investment and impact, and by having

Tip

The Quicker Map

If you already use cost centers or departments for your accounting system, this is a great starting point for discussion and can move the discussion along. Nevertheless, additional work will most likely need to be done to break out fund development programs. In your desire to speed up the process, don't forget to make sure that your strategic issue is reflected in your mission-specific and fund development programs.

OVERCOMING THE CHALLENGE

Why not map just mission-specific programs? Fundraising programs are there in support of them anyway. For nonprofits to be sustainable, they must meet the dual bottom line of impact and financial viability. Organizations that map only the mission-specific programs are missing the opportunity to integrate these two components and may not come up with a sustainable decision. Just mapping the mission-specific programs will not showcase a financially viable map. Therefore, both fund development programs and mission-specific programs need to be mapped to get a complete picture of the dual bottom line. In addition, organizations that effectively embrace a culture of philanthropy understand the power of using fund development programs not only to fund the organization but also in contributing to the organization's impact.

There are too many programs! It is no surprise to those of us working in the sector that even organizations with small budgets have a lot of activities and could easily have an unworkable number of programs. Larger organizations with multifaceted services face a similar challenge when trying to determine a meaningful number of programs to map. There is a tension between having a sufficient level of detail in your matrix map to provide meaningful guidance and the overall legibility of the matrix map. As with the question of program structure, make sure that your key strategic issues are reflected in whatever level of detail your map presents. Many organizations choose to collect detail on a large number of programs and then present the map in a consolidated manner. In doing so, when it comes time for analysis, you can dig down deeper in the data for additional guidance. Others have presented separate matrix maps for complex programs that have multiple components. As you think about the number of programs, consider the overarching structure of how your organization accomplishes its mission and the key drivers of impact and financial viability. These should be reflected in the first level of mission-specific and fund development programs.

separate programs for each, you'll be better positioned to determine where to invest to increase your organization's sustainability. Fund development programs tend to fall into some of the following categories:

+ Individual appeals
+ Major donors
+ Direct mail
+ Annual meeting
+ Special events
+ Unrestricted foundation funding
+ Corporate sponsorship

Impact and Revenue Strategies

Mission-specific programs tend to focus on how they contribute toward the desired organizational impact or their impact strategy. Similarly, when we consider a fund development program, we tend to think of how it generates resources or its revenue strategy. But because the matrix map explores the integration of the impact strategy and revenue strategy by looking collectively at the individual programs, it forces the recognition that each program has both a revenue strategy and an impact strategy. A revenue strategy is a means by which a particular program is financed. For mission-specific programs, that might mean charging a fee for service or securing restricted foundation grants. An impact strategy is the plan for the external effects to be sought through a particular program. Impact strategies for fund development programs may be to raise awareness of the mission or educate the public.

After the task force members identify the programs to map, they should identify the impact and revenue strategy for each program. This step can be done after the introductory meeting using the programs you've identified. Template 4.4

TEMPLATE 4.4 PROGRAMS, IMPACT, AND REVENUE STRATEGIES		
Mission-Specific and Fund Development Programs	**Impact Strategy**	**Revenue Strategy**

will help you with this process. (A completed example of this template is in table 4.1.) Have the person responsible for each program consider the impact and revenue strategy for his or her line and draft a statement to share at the next task force meeting. Identifying the programs and their respective impact and revenue strategies in this manner will help your thinking progress in this integrated fashion.

Table 4.1 Programs, Impact, and Revenue Strategies at Teen Parent Help

Mission-Specific and Fund Development Programs	Impact Strategy	Revenue Strategy
Adoption services	Connect loving parents with kids and babies in need of a home	Fees from prospective parents
Teen parenting	Prepare and support teenage parents for their new roles and responsibilities	Foundation support and city government support
Financial literacy	Education to help new parents make ends meet	Foundation grants and United Way support
Counseling	Emotional and psychological support for new teen parents	Health insurance and fee for service on a sliding scale
Individual appeals	Raise awareness of community issues around teenage pregnancy and solutions	Individual contributions
Special event	Entry-level awareness into the challenge of teenage pregnancy and unwanted babies	Ticket sales and sponsorships
Major donors	Raise awareness of issues affecting our local community around teenage pregnancy	Individual contributions

> ### OVERCOMING THE CHALLENGE: FINANCIAL INFORMATION
>
> One factor to consider when defining the structure of programs is the availability of financial information. Remember that you have to determine the profitability of every program you choose—both mission-specific and fund development programs. A template in chapter 5 can be used to determine profitability, but it is helpful to check in with your finance staff at this stage to determine how feasible it will be to obtain the financial information necessary to determine profitability.

Templates

Go to www.nonprofitsustainability.org for online access to the following templates from this chapter:

*   Task Force Meeting Agenda: Intended Impact and Programs: Sample agenda for the task force's articulation of intended impact and selection of programs to map
*   Intended Impact Survey: Questions to help articulate the organization's intended impact
*   Intended Impact Themes and Draft: A template to capture the discussion around intended impact and draft the organization's statement
*   Programs, Impact, and Revenue Strategies: A template to list your programs as well as their impact and revenue strategies

Summary

Even outside the matrix map process, understanding and articulating your organization's impact can be a valuable exercise. By focusing the organization on outcomes, the statement becomes a beacon of impact from which strategies and programs can flow. Once the statement is articulated and informed by the strategic issues, you then choose mission-specific and fund development programs that demonstrate how your organization accomplishes impact and generates revenue. Once you've chosen programs, articulate the impact and revenue strategies of each, bringing the dual-bottom-line theory to reality.

Assessing Mission Impact

CHAPTER

5

Mission impact is assessed for both the mission-specific and fund-development programs identified in chapter 4 and is done by rating or assessing each program on four criteria and then blending the scores to arrive at an overall mission impact score. The rigor and strategic utility of the matrix map process hinges substantially on the design and execution of the impact assessment process. When maps haven't had their desired effect, the reason is typically that the organization's leadership did not manage this process well. Too few staff and board had confidence in the resulting analysis, or the result wasn't challenging enough to the programmatic status quo to catalyze bold decision making. There are a number of critical choices that you'll make in this in this phase. In this chapter, we outline them and share our experiences of the opportunities and trade-offs in each (figure 5.1).

It is important to distinguish between designing the impact assessment process and executing it. Given that this is a subjective process by design—not an evaluation attempting to employ the scientific method—the potential for staff and

Figure 5.1 The Matrix Map Process: Assessing Mission Impact

board to feel confused, reticent, or even dubious is real. For many participants, the matrix map is the first time they have been asked to bring all of their knowledge, perspective, and opinion to bear in the relative assessment of existing programs. In our experience, you cannot take too much care in designing the process, including which stakeholders will or won't be involved and communicating your decisions clearly and frequently.

Process Overview

There are four steps the task force takes in designing the assessment process (figure 5.2):

1. Determine who will select and tailor the impact criteria.
2. Determine who will participate in the assessment.
3. Determine how the assessment will be conducted (e-survey or personal reflection with group discussion).
4. Communicate your design choices—actually, we recommend overcommunicating them—to everyone with any stake in the outcomes of this analysis.

Once the determinations are made, the five steps for executing the assessment process are taken (figure 5.3):

1. Select and tailor four impact criteria, the most essential elements of impact given your mission and current context.
2. Develop background material for mission-specific and fund development programs.
3. Create e-survey or assessment worksheets.

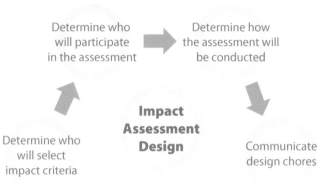

Figure 5.2 Sample Impact Assessment Design Overview

Figure 5.3 Impact Assessment Execution Overview

4. Conduct assessment.
5. Discuss assessment results.

Designing the Impact Assessment

Similar to deciding on your programmatic structure that we discussed in chapter 4, the task force has many choices to make in designing the impact assessment. It is important to answer them thoughtfully, paying attention to how your choices will resonate with the full staff and board and infuse the process with credibility.

Determine Who Will Select and Tailor the Impact Criteria

Choosing and tailoring the impact criteria is one of the most strategic aspects of the entire matrix map process. For a group of people to determine together that four elements of impact matter the most for the organization given everything they know about the internal and external environments at the moment is a powerful exercise.

Many organizations tend to move quickly into selecting criteria to assess mission impact, but it is worth pausing to make sure the correct group is making that decision. In many cases, it will be the same task force established for the overall matrix map process. However, depending on the size and culture of the organization, the task force may decide that engaging a broader group in this discussion will add value or foster greater buy-in to the ultimate results.

A crucial consideration in deciding who should select the criteria is whether you intend to have a larger group than the task force participate in the assessment itself. If so, think carefully about the climate in your organization and whether non–task force members will engage fully with criteria that they did not help select. As always, the key here is communication and transparency.

A crucial consideration in deciding who should select the criteria is whether you intend to have a larger group than the task force participate in the assessment itself.

Determine Who Will Participate in the Assessment

Beyond selecting the criteria, there is the decision to be made of who will be conducting the assessment. This choice is about ensuring rounded, quality input and in some ways is a tension between broad input with limited knowledge or less input with more in-depth knowledge. The goal is to ensure that a broad range of proximities to and perspectives on both the mission-specific and fund development programs is included. A smaller group may allow a more in-depth discussion and analysis. However, it also opens up the process to complaints that others were excluded. The concern that arises is the degree to which some potential participants are familiar with only some aspects of the organization. In general, we recommend pushing past this concern in the dual interests of engaging more voices and educating more people, through their participation, about the system as a whole. This decision is closely tied to the choice of assessment method. In our experience, if there will be an anonymous e-survey of all asked to complete the assessment to score the impact of each program, you need to be more concerned about the knowledge base of each participant. If, however, you are going to use the personal reflection with group discussion method, you can trust to some degree that the group process will correct for individuals' blind spots during the reflection process.

Determine How the Assessment Will Be Conducted

There are two common methods for conducting the assessment. One is to create an e-survey that each participant completes on his or her own, with the results tallied and averaged by one of the task force members or the consultant if one is involved. The other method is to hold an in-person discussion where the results of the assessment and the reasoning behind them are openly shared resulting in shared learning and eventually coming to a mutual decision about the mission impact score for each program.

The advantage of an e-survey is anonymity, which may ensure that participants feel safe in providing their honest assessments of each program without the pressure of their peers hearing and judging their answers. There are three situations where this may be the best course of action:

+ When trust among participants generally, or in senior management specifically, is low
+ When the stakes are high and fairly immediate, for example, in a financial crisis where this process is being used to select programs for elimination
+ When distance, staff or board size, or other logistical factors make it more practical

The trade-off is that participants miss an opportunity to discuss their reasoning behind each score, educate one another from their unique vantage points, and influence one another's thinking. This is the distinct advantage of the personal reflection with group discussion method described later in this chapter, which on balance we prefer in organizations where it is feasible. We think this approach leads to more accurate scores. Instead of one participant's score of 4 and one participant's score of 1 for a given criterion and program being averaged to a 2.5, which captures neither of their intentions, through debate and discussion the group can arrive at its actual score. Moreover, these discussions are among the most transformative of the process when a group of people has been well prepared for them and is facilitated to have them courageously, with all participants sharing their knowledge of the programs' impact candidly. The shared analyses they establish live on long past the creation of the matrix map.

These discussions are among the most transformative of the process when a group of people has been well prepared for them and is facilitated to have them courageously, with all participants sharing their knowledge of the programs' impact candidly.

Communicate Your Design Choices

Once the task force makes its decisions, it needs to communicate them to both board and staff. If people across the staff and board are to embrace the matrix map's

Tip

The Quicker Map

This is not an area to shortchange. Assessing mission impact is at the crux of the matrix map. Because of the subjective nature of the assessment, it is worth spending more time here to make sure that key stakeholders understand and agree with the decisions made.

messages and participate fully in developing and implementing follow-on actions, it is critical that they have faith in the process from start to finish. We recommend clearly distinguishing between the matrix map process design, implementation, and interpretation (see the next chapter) phases and communicating decisions about who will be involved when and why at every step along the way.

Template 5.1 will help you keep track of the decisions that have been made so far. After you've designed the process, it is time to begin implementation and assess the programs.

TEMPLATE 5.1 MATRIX MAP PROCESS DECISIONS	
Area	**Decision**
Mission-specific programs	
Fund development programs	
Who is defining mission impact criteria?	
Who is assessing mission impact of programs?	
Who is responsible for communication?	

Implementing the Assessment Process

Once the mission impact process is designed, it is time to implement it. We begin with one of the more important decisions: selecting the criteria that comprise the impact score of the programs.

Select the Impact Criteria

Choosing impact criteria that challenge staff and board to assess the current state of affairs against what they know or imagine to be emerging practice—as opposed to the existing standard practice—results in a far more useful assessment process. The worst-case scenario is a matrix map that affirms stale practices rather than one that stirs leaders to push for the change in program mix, design, or execution that will increase mission relevance and impact.

In *Nonprofit Sustainability*, we offered seven nonprofit impact elements: aligned with core mission, scale, depth, excellence in execution, filling an important gap, community building, and leverage.[1] These elements are the explicit rationale for an activity's inclusion in the business model. No organization can do everything that is potentially needed or aligned with its mission; strategy is about making choices about the set of activities that will drive impact as the organization currently defines it and ensure its financial viability.

In this book, we are making two significant shifts to our recommended practice of selecting impact criteria. These shifts, based on our consulting with leaders across all mission types and budget sizes, are intended to ensure that your map is rigorous and useful in strategic decision making. First, we reconceived and renamed the criterion that we referred to as "alignment with core mission." The fact is that very few nonprofits do things that are counter to their missions. Mission statements tell us what *not* to do (something off mission), but they do not tell us what we *should* do to best achieve the impact we seek on our issue or with our constituencies. Whereas mission has been the traditional organizing principle in our sector, it has given way to impact.

The second shift is that we now suggest that all groups use two criteria— contribution to intended impact and excellence in execution—and then select two from the remaining five that are most relevant to their organization's strategic priorities and direction. These two criteria are fundamental to good programming regardless of organizational type. Again, referring to Jim Collin's flywheel concept, if something does not drive toward the change we want to see—whether that change is exceptional live theater or comprehensive immigration reform—there is no reason it should be in our model.[2] And just as important, if we cannot achieve

Whereas mission has been the traditional organizing principle in our sector, it has given way to impact.

greatness at something that is very important, then why not let others who can step in. These standards of relevance and excellence seem inherently nonnegotiable to us.

Below we define further the two mandatory criteria and the five optional criteria from which to choose. Because we have found that some groups benefit from tailoring the language of the criteria to fit their particular notions of impact or relevance, we also offer an example of such tailoring in each case.

Criterion 1: Contribution to Intended Impact—Mandatory

Here you will be referring directly to the work you did in step 2 of the matrix map process: articulate intended impact. By focusing on intended impact rather than mission, the task force is creating the space for an important and exciting conversation about how the organization may want to revisit the design of one or more programs. A program that remains completely aligned with mission may nonetheless benefit immensely from a team of staff, clients, and volunteers radically reconsidering its design toward a more current notion of impact. Many fields are going through major reassessments of what impact looks like—think of "rapid rehousing" instead of shelters, or the performing arts as community engagement experiences rather than passive audience experiences. And in these fields, the work of bringing donors along and engaging them in new thinking too is critical to viability. In short, the discussion of this criterion can spur needed innovation.

> *Tailored example for a domestic violence organization:* "To what extent, as it's currently executed, does this program promote a violence-free community for our clients and donors?"

Criterion 2: Excellence in Execution—Mandatory

This criterion is a direct challenge to traditional notions of nonprofit strategy wherein many leaders assumed that if a program was needed and mission aligned,

A program that remains completely aligned with mission may nonetheless benefit immensely from a team of staff, clients, and volunteers radically reconsidering its design toward a more current notion of impact.

A NOTE ABOUT RELATIVE SCORING

Assessing mission impact is an exercise in both absolute and relative scoring, especially with contribution to intended impact and excellence in execution. *Absolute scoring* takes a look at each mission-specific and fund development program and asks how it individually performs on the criteria. Is this something our organization does well? *Relative scoring* assesses the programs relative to other programs that the organization offers. For example, you may be excellent at your outreach program, but what is truly a core competency and competitive strategic advantage when compared to other organizations is your counseling service. From an absolute perspective, you might rate outreach high, but when you consider it relative to your other programs, you might lower the score just a little bit. This is not to say that you can't have two programs with the same score but just that it is important to look at them in the context of the organization as a whole to end up with meaningful data and differences.

it should stay in the business model at any cost. Today, with a new focus on impact, it is not enough for a program to be aligned with intended impact; the nonprofit has to be doing it well to be of service to its communities and causes. This is the criterion that allows a group of leaders to bring to the assessment discussion not theory or ideals, but the actual experience—smooth or fraught—of delivering a program day in and day out. Here, issues of client engagement and results, donor or funder loyalty, caliber of staff, and strength of systems are raised. So often strategic planning is a forward-looking and theoretical exercise, when in fact the proverbial plane is in flight and what is needed as much as compelling strategy is exceptional execution. Nonprofits that sustain theoretically relevant but poorly executed programs are doing harm by underserving their constituents and, in cases where there are other provider options, absorbing financial resources that could be better deployed elsewhere. This criterion should surface any such uncomfortable truths.

> *Tailored example from a community clinic:* "To what extent, as it's currently executed, does this program fully employ our current organizational systems and protocols for optimally supporting clients and donors?"

Criterion 3: Scale

For some organizations, the extent of their reach is a critical element of their intended impact. *Scale* can refer to the number of people served by a program or exposed to a campaign; it can refer to the number of population groups or communities reached; and it can refer to growth trajectories if an organization is in a formal scaling-up process. The caution here is that nearly all organizations count participants and donors, so that data feel more relevant than they may in fact be for the purposes of the matrix map. Encourage the selection of this criterion if your organization has active, strategic, and relative questions about the scale of its programs.

> *Tailored example from a food bank:* "To what extent, as it's currently executed, does this program reach the breadth of diverse client and donor families in our community?"

Criterion 4: Depth

Many organizations intentionally have a mix of breadth and depth in their program portfolios. They may do immigration-related media seen by thousands and long-term case management with one hundred undocumented families per year, for instance. *Depth* can refer to the relative length of participants' engagement, the intensity of a program's design or methodology, and the degree of transformation experienced by clients or participants. For groups grappling with the transformative impact of traditional social services (see chapter 1), this criterion is often tailored to explore how deeply engaged they are with their constituents in their current program models. In most cases, depth is about getting past the inputs (e.g., meals served) to the outcomes (e.g., eating habits changed). In the fund development context, it could refer to retention of donors rather than transient acquisition.

> *Tailored example from a racial justice organization:* "To what extent, as it's currently executed, does this program result in lasting, attitudinal shifts about racism among our participants and donors?"

Criterion 5: Significant Unmet Need

For some nonprofits, responding to unmet needs is a recurring strategic principle. Some organizations are the only providers of a program or service in a given area or for a certain segment of the population. Others may have peer organizations but know that the demand for services is greater than their combined capacity. Unmet need is a dynamic reality, so this may be an appropriate criterion if leadership senses important shifts. The implementation of the Affordable Care Act is a good example. For many years, community-based health organizations have filled a service gap for low-income and underserved community members, many of whom now theoretically have access to the mainstream health care system. Certainly, having a current sense of the provider landscape is crucial when employing this criterion; the changing landscape may be particularly less visible to board members, for instance, so educating them during this process is important.

Not unlike the Scale criterion, we caution leaders from selecting Significant Unmet Need unless responding to scarcity is core to their organizational strategy *and* they have active and relative questions about the extent to which their programs are still among the only viable options for their constituents. If not, this criterion can be a wasted, "feel-good" choice that doesn't yield strategic analysis for

Unmet need is a dynamic reality, so this may be an appropriate criterion if leadership senses important shifts.

decision making. Put simply, if you know you are the only game in town, why use the matrix map process to affirm that?

> *Tailored example from a rural family support center:* "To what extent, as it's currently executed, is this program our participants' only option of its kind in this community?"

Criterion 6: Community Building

Nonprofits are not only about their provision of a service, their performance of a play, or their advocacy for a particular issue. They are often also significant centers of civic engagement and nurturers of communities, geographic or otherwise. For some nonprofits, these roles are integral to how they do their work. In such cases, community building is often a resonant impact criterion. It can refer to the extent that the community is engaged in the delivery of a program, the power of convening, or the level of inclusion a program fosters among an often isolated group or population.

> *Tailored example from community child care center:* "To what extent, as it's currently executed, does this program meaningfully connect the current families, alumni, and community around our school?"

Criterion 7: Leverage

Organizations are systems that operate in numerous larger systems. In an increasingly networked world, they have to create leverage in how they nurture the intersections between people and programs and how they contribute to and benefit from any number of partnerships inside and outside their organizations. Leverage can manifest in a basic-needs drop-in center that offers the opportunity for clients to view artwork and sign up for an art class, a coalition that gets senior staff a seat at the table with funders and allies, a co-location that means students don't have to leave their school campus to get counseling services, and so on. If creating and sustaining leverage is paramount in the strategic choices that an organization makes, this criterion will be relevant. It is especially resonant for advocacy and coalition-building organizations that are fundamentally dependent on the strength of their partnerships. And it may be relevant for an organization working to integrate its own people and programming, essentially calling out the relative degree of isolation or interdependence of each program as currently executed.

> *Tailored example from a youth mentoring program:* "To what extent, as it's currently executed, does this program effectively leverage our partnerships with business and civic leaders?"

Craft Strong Criteria

The quality of the impact assessment is dependent on the quality of the criteria used, so in this case, robust discussions, and even wordsmithing are called for. There are the three keys to developing strong criteria:

1. *Link criteria to strategic questions.* Use the strategic issues that are facing the organization identified in the introductory meeting to inform the selection and tailoring of criteria. If you don't have a question about the scale of your programs, why assess it unless it is a core value of the organization? Rigorous and contextualized criteria will yield the best conversations and the most strategic decision making down the road. Remember that the matrix map is not a public document like a strategic plan often is. The aim is not to score high on everything; on the contrary, the objective is to identify what matters most to the organization's impact today and conduct an honest self-assessment of what is relevant and on target, and where there is room for change or improvement.

Rigorous and contextualized criteria will yield the best conversations and the most strategic decision making down the road.

2. *Craft single-issue criteria.* Make each criterion a singular idea so that it can be assessed consistently by all participants. In the example below, I might feel that some programs do an excellent job of building connections among community members, but do not in fact increase their likelihood of lifelong participation in

local elections, or vice versa. I can only provide an accurate score for a single impact element, not a compound one.

> *Wrong:* "To what extent, as currently executed, does this program build connections among community members and increase their likelihood of lifelong participation in local elections."
>
> *Right—option 1:* "To what extent, as currently executed, does this program build connections among community members?"
>
> *Right—option 2:* "To what extent, as currently executed, does this program promote participants' and donors' lifelong participation in local elections?"

3. *Pretest the criteria language.* Test the criteria language on a cross-section of staff and board before conducting the assessment to ensure that you can explain it consistently verbally and in writing and that people understand it. Think of this as you would user testing you would conduct on any survey before a data collection process. It will be too late if you get back weak survey results or have a disappointing group discussion because participants had inconsistent understandings of what the criteria meant and how to apply them.

To assist you in choosing criteria, template 5.2 provides a list of all the criteria for you to distribute to the group selecting the criteria.

Tip

The Quicker Map

If your organization has prepared a matrix map before, it may make sense to start with the criteria you used previously and determine if they still apply to your strategic issues. If so, you may go ahead and use them again to save time.

CHOOSING YOUR OWN CRITERIA

The seven criteria are the overarching impact themes that are most often used for organizations. Of course, if your organization has different criteria that are more clearly related to your strategic issues, you should feel free to come up with your own. Often this can be done by tailoring one of the seven criteria already listed, but it may be something completely different. For example, an organization that is trying to work more collectively with others added a criterion around partnership and collaboration.

TEMPLATE 5.2   MISSION IMPACT CRITERIA

Potential Criteria	Definition
Contribution to intended impact	Relative to other programs, how well does this program contribute to what the overall organization aims accomplish?
Excellence in execution	Is this program something that the organization delivers in an exceptional manner?
Scale	How many people are touched or influenced by this program?
Depth	How profound is the level of intervention with this program?
Significant unmet need	Is there significant competition, or are there similar offerings of this program? Is there an adequate supply of services to meet the demand for them in our community?
Community building	Does this program build community around the program or the organization as a whole?
Leverage	Does this program benefit from and nurture important relationships and partnerships inside and outside the organization?

Develop Background Material for Mission-Specific and Fund Development Programs

We ask all participants to bring their full knowledge and experience with a program into the assessment process. However, it is only natural with a diverse group of participants that each will have differing levels of knowledge about each individual program. Board members especially tend to have uneven knowledge across all of the mission-specific and fund development programs. This is more of a reflection of the structure of board meetings and their interests than anything else. For example, a newer program may be discussed in depth at the board level at the expense of an existing, quality program that may not have issues that rise to the board's attention. In the same way, certain fund development programs garner more attention because of the board's involvement than others. To provide a baseline of knowledge, template 5.3 provides an overview of each program for your participants. Each program's manager should complete this template prior

TEMPLATE 5.3   PROGRAM OVERVIEW

Program Name	Comments
Number of people touched in past year:	
Funding streams:	
In a single sentence, what is being offered with this program?	
Who benefits from or who is target audience for the program?	
How deep is our involvement with the constituent in this program?	
Is this program something we do exceptionally do? How so? How do we define exceptional performance?	
Are there other organizations or competitors that offer something similar to this program?	
How does this program help build community around the organization?	

to the assessment and for both mission-specific and fund development programs. The template can be modified depending on the criteria selected to be used for the assessment. This brief document provides some basic information and should be as objective as possible, allowing readers to interpret and add their own judgments.

Create the E-Survey or Assessment Worksheets

Whether you are creating an electronic survey or worksheets for individual reflection prior to a group discussion, the essential structure is the same. Provide a cover sheet of instruction and definitions to reground participants in what they are being asked to do, encourage their thoughtfulness and candor, and set their expectations for the next steps in the process.

For each of the four criteria, provide a worksheet or e-survey section that lists every mission-specific and fundraising program and provides a Likert scale of 1 to 4 and a space for notes and reflections. If you have determined that some participants are so unfamiliar with one or more programs that they cannot provide useful data, you can include a "don't know" option, with very clear instructions of when it is appropriate to use it. Table 5.1 is a sample assessment sheet, and template 5.4 can be used to for your own assessment. You will have four worksheets—one for each criterion—for every participant.

Conduct the Assessment

If you have elected to use an electronic survey, build it in an online tool such as SurveyMonkey or SurveyGizmo and distribute it electronically to participants. Determine who will manage the survey, and tally the averages for each program line. If you are using the personal reflection and group discussion method, distribute the packet of instructions and four worksheets (one for each criterion) to all

Table 5.1 Sample Assessment Worksheet/E-Survey Page					
To what extent, as it's currently executed, does this program meaningfully engage our members and volunteers in its delivery?	**1 (Not at All)**	**2**	**3**	**4 (Very Much)**	**Don't Know**
A. Drop-in resource center Notes:					
B. Financial literacy Notes:					
C. Job placement Notes:					
D. Mentoring: Notes:					
E. Annual donor campaign Notes:					
F. Annual jobs fair and corporate sponsors' dinner Notes:					

TEMPLATE 5.4   SAMPLE ASSESSMENT INTRODUCTION AND WORKSHEET OR E-SURVEY PAGE

Introduction

This survey is part of the matrix map framework for better understanding and strengthening our organization's business model. In doing so, we look at how both our mission-specific and fund development programs contribute to the impact and financial viability of our organization.

This survey is designed to assess the mission impact of each of our organization's programs. Some background on the programs is provided in the program overview [*if your organization has completed this document*].

In this assessment, we assess both programmatic and fundraising activities because each activity, regardless of its primary function, has both an impact and a financial component. Put another way, our fundraising activities help accomplish our mission beyond simply raising money—they also raise awareness and understanding, which is part of our mission impact.

Mission impact will be a blended score based on four criteria:

[*Summarize criteria here*]

We will describe each of these criteria in more detail as we move through the survey.

As you take the survey, we ask that you call on your individual judgment based on your perceptions and data that you are familiar with. For some questions, you may not feel qualified to make an assessment; nevertheless, your position as a stakeholder of the organization makes your perceptions particularly valuable.

Also, please think about the relative impact of the programs. Certainly everything we do has impact, so as you look at the list, ask yourself, "Which has the most impact?" or, "Do all of these have the same impact?" and rate the programs appropriately.

Your honest candor is greatly appreciated and will be most helpful in moving our discussions and, ultimately, our organization forward.

Thank you again for your time. If you have any questions, please feel free to contact our task force.

Assessment Worksheet/E-Survey Page

Program
Criterion

Criterion 1:	**1 (Not at All)**	**2**	**3**	**4 (Very Much)**	**Don't Know**
A. Program A:					
Notes:					
Criterion 1:	**1 (Not at All)**	**2**	**3**	**4 (Very Much)**	**Don't Know**
B. Program B:					
Notes:					
Criterion 1:	**1 (Not at All)**	**2**	**3**	**4 (Very Much)**	**Don't Know**
C. Program C:					
Notes:					
Criterion 1:	**1 (Not at All)**	**2**	**3**	**4 (Very Much)**	**Don't Know**
D. Program D:					
Notes:					
Criterion 1:	**1 (Not at All)**	**2**	**3**	**4 (Very Much)**	**Don't Know**
E. Program E:					
Notes:					
Criterion 1:	**1 (Not at All)**	**2**	**3**	**4 (Very Much)**	**Don't Know**
F. Program F:					
Notes:					

participants. Set a meeting time for a week to two weeks after the distribution for all participants to come together to discuss their scores. If the organization has numerous distinct programs, you may decide to schedule two group discussions to ensure that people are fresh for the totality of the dialogue.

We have facilitated very powerful group discussions in this format. Template 5.5 provides a typical agenda for these meetings, which generally follows this example:

A. Review the matrix map process: Where are we in the process? What comes next?

B. Check in on the experience of the personal impact assessment: Hear from each person on the experience of the assessment—his or her challenges and insights

C. Criterion 1/program 1

   a. Each participant has 2 minutes to share his or her score and reasoning.

   b. After hearing from everyone, the facilitator reads back the scores and looks for movement or consensus if there is variance—for example, "We have four 4s and one 2. [To the colleague who gave this program a 2:] Have you been influenced by the group, or do you wish to make another argument for your lower score?" And so on. You don't have to come to consensus, but it is nice if you can. If not, you go with the score the majority of participants gave.

D. Repeat C for program 2 through all the programs.

E. Repeat C and D for criteria 2 to 4.

F. Discuss themes: What issues came up repeatedly? Where did we have the most agreement? Where was there divergent thinking? What do we view as the three to five initial impact messages from our matrix map process?

TEMPLATE 5.5   MISSION IMPACT ASSESSMENT MEETING AGENDA

Mission Impact Assessment

Goals

- Discuss and assess the mission impact of each mission-specific and fund development program along the four criteria.

- Determine the mission impact score for each program.

Agenda

- Review the matrix map process

- Check-in on personal impact assessment
  - Challenges
  - Insights

- Explain the process for sharing scores: "We'll take each criterion and go program by program. Each person will have up to two minutes to talk about why he or she gave it that score."

- Criterion 1: Contribution to Intended Impact
  - Program 1
  - Program 2
  - Program 3
  - Program 4
  - Program 5

- Criterion 2: Excellence in execution
  - Program 1
  - Program 2
  - Program 3
  - Program 4
  - Program 5

- Criterion 3
  - Program 1
  - Program 2
  - Program 3
  - Program 4
  - Program 5

- Criterion 4
  - Program 1
  - Program 2
  - Program 3
  - Program 4
  - Program 5

- Themes

- Determine Score

- Next steps

With your scores determined by either e-survey or group discussion, a task force member creates the score averages that will be entered into the matrix map template. Typically this is done by averaging the four scores for each program. However, some task forces decide that their impact criteria are of differing significance so they weight them accordingly. Here is an example of how this works:

Mentoring Program (Nonweighted)	
Contribution to intended impact	4
Excellence in execution	2
Depth	3
Community building	3
Matrix map impact average score	3

Mentoring Program (Weighted)	
Contribution to intended impact (40%)	4
Excellence in execution (40%)	2
Depth (10%)	3
Community building (10%)	3
Matrix map impact weighted score	3

Template 5.6 provides two sheets to keep track of mission impact scores during the discussion and to calculate the overall mission impact score.

TEMPLATE 5.6   MISSION IMPACT SCORE SHEET

Assessing Mission Impact
Criterion:

Program	1	2	3	4	5	6	7	8	9	10	11	12	13	14	15	16	17	18	19	20	Average
Program 1																					
Program 2																					
Program 3																					
Program 4																					
Program 5																					
Program 6																					
Program 7																					
Program 8																					

Assessing Mission Impact
Weighted Mission Impact

Weights	0.25	0.25	0.25	0.25	
	Criterion 1: Contribution to Intended Impact	**Criterion 2: Excellence in Execution**	**Criterion 3:**	**Criterion 4:**	**Mission Impact**
Program 1					
Program 2					
Program 3					
Program 4					
Program 5					
Program 6					
Program 7					
Program 8					

Templates

Go to www.nonprofitsustainability.org for online access to the following templates from this chapter:

- Matrix Map Process Decisions: For keeping track of decisions made to assess mission impact
- Mission Impact Criteria: List of criteria to choose from
- Program Overview: To provide an overview of each program and aid in assessment
- Sample Assessment Introduction and Worksheet or E-Survey: Distributed to participants to gather their assessments of the programs for each criterion
- Mission Impact Assessment Meeting Agenda: Sample agenda for the meeting to discuss the mission impact scores
- Mission Impact Score Sheet: To help determine the mission impact of each program

Summary

A rigorous process for assessing mission impact is essential for a meaningful matrix map. We broke this step down into two parts: designing the impact assessment and implementing the impact assessment. Designing the assessment entails deciding who will participate in selecting criteria and assessing impact, as well as what process will be used to capture the assessment. It also entails communicating and sharing information frequently to build trust for the process. Implementing the impact assessment starts with combining the two mandatory criteria with two selected from the remaining optional criteria and tailoring them to capture the strategic issues your organization is facing. Assessment can be done by e-survey or by in-person discussion, but the results should be shared and discussed before the average is taken for each program across the four criteria to arrive at the final mission impact score.

Determining Profitability

After navigating through the subjective, and for some uncomfortable, conversations about mission impact, profitability seemingly provides an oasis of objective data. But as accountants will tell you, by the time you're done with allocating all the costs and revenue streams to specific business lines, objectivity is an illusion. Not to worry. In this chapter, we walk you step-by-step through how to determine the profitability of your programs (figure 6.1).

Profitability is essential for nonprofits to be financially viable and sustainable, yet there sometimes lingers the archaic notion that nonprofits can't, or shouldn't, be profitable. Yet like any other business, a nonprofit organization needs to be profitable to secure its future. Senior leaders and board members sometimes bristle at the word *profitability*, because they think it implies a focus solely on profitability or that every program needs to be profitable. Neither of these is true. Not every program within a nonprofit can be profitable. Often organizations are founded because of market failure: there is a need for a service without a possible payer. In other cases, revenue may cover a portion of the total expenses, but not enough to break even. In the dual-bottom-line model, however, these programs may be essential for their contribution to the organization's overall impact. Looking at them not individually but in relation to the financial profitability of other programs, both mission-specific and fund development programs, is essential.

Figure 6.1   The Matrix Map Process: Determining Profitability

For every program that can't break even, another needs to generate a surplus if the organization is to be viable.

Although not every program needs to be profitable, some need to be for the organization to be financially sustainable. The matrix map is about balance. For every program that can't break even, another needs to generate a surplus if the organization is to be viable.

To be sustainable, nonprofits need to have some years when the organization as a whole is profitable. Profitability builds operating reserves, which allows organizations to invest in new, potentially higher-impact ideas before they have support from foundations or the marketplace. They also allow organizations to survive in economic downturns, maintaining services while adjusting their business models.

Pairing profitability with impact in the matrix map creates a way of thinking of the return on investment. The matrix map demonstrates how much impact an organization is having for the total expenses, both direct programmatic and indirect administrative expenses, invested into the program. The goal over the course of building sustainability is to maximize that impact or return in a financially viable manner. The matrix map and the resulting strategic decisions help to accomplish this goal.

A strong financial structure and systems are important for leading your organization regardless of whether you are creating a matrix map, but they will especially help as part of this process. In this chapter, we offer a primer on nonprofit finance and a step-by-step guide for determining the profitability of your program. If you have a sophisticated accounting system and structure, you may find it a good refresher but might not need to follow each of the steps. However, it still may be worth a quick review to make sure that you have profitability correctly established for each of the organization's programs.

Let's start with better understanding the expense side of your organization.

Nonprofit Expenses

Thinking about profitability and financial sustainability begins with an understanding of what resources are required to create impact and run the organization. Start by determining the true costs of operating each mission-specific and fund development program: direct expenses, shared expenses, and a portion of administrative expenses.

Direct expenses are those costs incurred by and directly attributable to a program. For example, a nutrition education program might have direct expenses of printing for the curriculum, flip charts, and paper for training, and perhaps food for samples. Direct expenses for a direct mail program might include copy writing, printing, and postage. The relationship between the expense and the program is typically clear, and direct expenses tend to be coded directly to a program in the accounting system. (*Programs* and *cost centers* may be synonymous here. Although mission-specific programs are typically broken down in the accounting system, it is rare that fund development programs are broken down with this level of specificity in the accounting system.)

Unlike direct expenses, shared expenses (also called *shared costs* or *common costs*) don't relate to one specific program but rather are shared among multiple mission-specific and fund development programs. These are typically occupancy expenses such as rent, utilities, and insurance. They can also include some personnel expenses for positions that work directly with multiple mission-specific and fund development programs, such as the office manager. They also commonly include technology-related expenses such as the Internet, a computer specialist in the office, or e-mail-related expenses. Although these expenses directly benefit specific programs, it would be tedious and cumbersome to identify the exact portion of the expense that is attributable to each program. Therefore, we group them together as a shared expense and then allocate or split them out based on a methodology called a cost allocation basis.

The most common cost allocation basis used to split shared expenses is full-time equivalents (FTEs). Under this method, shared expenses are split among programs based on the percentage of total full-time employees (or the equivalent thereof) that are working for the program. For example, consider a mission-specific program with the following personnel:

+ One-fourth of the executive director's time
+ One-half of the program director's time
+ One social worker
+ Three part-time case managers working a twenty-hour week (1.5 FTEs)

We'd add the portion of everyone's time together to determine the full-time equivalents for this department, which would be 3.25. If there were 10 FTEs in the organization among all the mission-specific and fund development programs, this program would receive 32.5 percent (3.25/10) of all the shared expenses. When you think about full-time equivalents as a cost allocation basis, it makes logical sense. Programs with more staff typically use more space and technology by virtue of having more people and therefore account for more of the expenses. We'll explain a little bit more about how to determine this allocation when we look at the staffing plan next.

Most nonfinance staff are unaware of shared costs because accounting systems allocate them to individual programs at the time invoices are entered based on established percentages. For our purposes, the most important point is that each program should have a portion of occupancy, technology, and other expenses because they are vital for their operation and part of the true costs of the program.

The third expense category for a nonprofit organization, after direct and shared expenses, is administrative expenses—those costs required to keep the organization's corporate legal status. (See figure 6.2.) They include accounting expenses, audit fees, and time spent with the board of directors. Although items like rent and technology may appear administrative in nature, they are not classified entirely as administrative expenses. Rather, they are classified as shared costs and then allocated to all activities including administration. This is true not only for the matrix map process but also for audited financial statements and IRS Form 990.

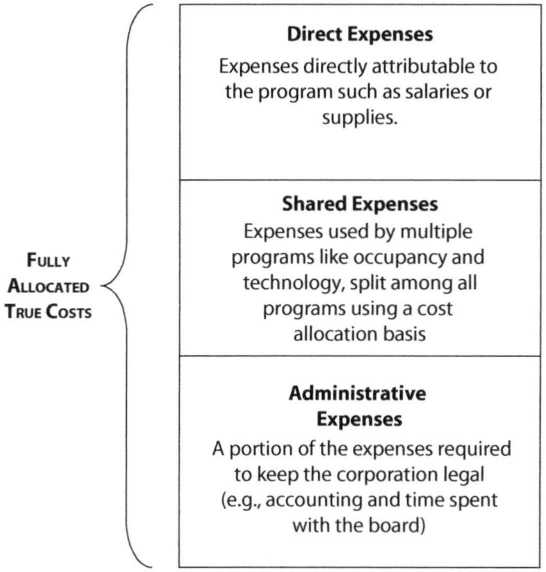

Correctly categorizing expenses into direct, shared, or administrative is the foundation for all financial reporting. While coding expenses can be one of the least fun tasks of nonprofit management, it is essential to produce meaningful reports that enable you to lead your organization towards sustainability.

Figure 6.2 Nonprofit Expenses

Staffing Plan

Coding expenses such as meals or supplies to the appropriate program may be straightforward, but when it comes to splitting payroll expenses of stretched nonprofit staff who work in several areas, it can cause a conundrum. Because payroll and personnel-related expenses are typically the highest expenses for nonprofit organizations, determining where people are spending their time is essential for understanding the true cost of delivering the mission. To do this, we create a staffing plan spreadsheet. A sample is shown in exhibit 6.1 and is also available as template 6.1.

Exhibit 6.1 Sample Staffing Plan

Rivers for All

Staffing Plan

Position	% FTE	Mission-Specific Programs				Fund Development Programs					
		Water Quality Monitoring	Training & Education	Community Engagement	Advocacy	Unrestricted Foundations	Membership	Events	Admin.	Shared	Total
Executive Director	100%	5%	10%	10%	15%	13%	12%	10%	25%		1.00
Program Director	100%	5%	20%	20%	50%				5%		1.00
Finance Director	50%								50%		0.50
Outreach Coordinator	100%		20%	35%		5%	15%	10%	15%		1.00
Water Quality Specialist	100%	60%	30%		10%						1.00
Water Quality Specialist	100%	50%	50%								1.00
Water Quality Specialist	100%	50%			50%						1.00
Development Coordinator	25%					16%	1%	6%	1%		0.25
Total	6.75	1.70	1.30	0.65	1.25	0.34	0.28	0.26	0.96	–	6.75
Total Less Shared	6.75										
Shared Allocation %		25%	19%	10%	19%	5%	4%	4%	14%	−100%	

The staffing plan lists each of the programs across the top and each employee's name or position down the first column. The second column reflects the percent of time they work. An executive director working full time will be at 100 percent. In exhibit 6.1, the finance director works half-time and is listed at 50 percent.

TEMPLATE 6.1 STAFFING PLAN										
		Mission-Specific Programs				Fund Development Programs				
Employee/Position	% FTE	1	2	3	4	5	6	Shared Costs	Admin.	Total Time

Total time:

Total less shared

Shared allocation: Total time/Total less shared

Once the employee listing is established, split their time between the mission-specific and fund development programs. Employees who work in only one area can easily have their total time put under that program, but the process will be more nuanced for senior managers or others who split their time among several programs. Organizations that receive government contracts will most likely have timesheets for employees that can be referred to during this part of the process. If you don't have timesheets, have a conversation with staff about where they spend their time and make an estimate to complete the staffing plan.

THE EXECUTIVE DIRECTOR'S TIME IN SHARED COSTS

Since the executive director's time is often split throughout the organization, we are regularly asked about whether that time should be put entirely into administration or allocated out as a shared expense. It certainly is understandable to think of the executive director's time as an administrative activity, since he or she spends a significant amount of time working with the board and fundraising. However, in most organizations, the executive director also works directly in programs either as a program manager in smaller organizations or working with staff to figure out the program's strategy. In some cases, the executive director is even engaged in direct service. This split may call for his or her salary to be allocated as a shared expense, but we encourage you to be more systematic. Take the time to ask where the executive director is truly spending his or her time. Look at his or her calendar for the last several weeks and see if that gives you a hint of the breakdown. Come up with a specific split for the executive director based on your organization. Even your best guess will provide a more accurate assessment of the payroll split and therefore a more accurate estimate of your full costs and profitability.

OVERCOMING THE CHALLENGE: DETERMINING EXPENSES OF FUND DEVELOPMENT PROGRAMS

Even for sophisticated organizations, the process of determining expenses for individual fund development programs is not very common. This level of detail is not typically kept in accounting systems where financial statements merely report fundraising as a cumulative reflection of all efforts. For purposes of the matrix map, it is best to break fund development down into individual programs like direct mail, major gifts, and special events. This means an extra layer of analysis is required in determining profitability, but with the systems in place that we described above, it should not be hard to do.

Using the staffing plan, sit with staff who perform fund development (including the executive director) and determine where they spend their time. If, for example, they spend time writing a government contract for a health clinic business line, that time should be put under that program. We know that the government contract won't cover the fundraising cost, but it is a valid expense for operating that program and should be included within that program. On the other hand, even if a mission-specific program is used as the pitch for an unrestricted gift through direct mail, their time should be put toward direct mail.

After allocating payroll expenses, perform the same task with any other direct expenses that development might incur. In doing so you'll now have the direct costs of each of the fund development programs.

Once the staffing plan is completed, it can be easily linked to a worksheet that will calculate the personnel expense per program. A sample is shown in exhibit 6.2. The percentage of time under each mission-specific and fund development program for each employee is multiplied by the employee's total salary to come up with the salary expense for the program (template 6.2).

Beyond using the staffing plan to determine the personnel expenses for each program, it can also be used to determine the cost allocation basis by which you allocate shared expenses. This method of allocation would be based on the FTEs who work in each mission-specific and fund development program. At the bottom of the staffing plan, as shown in exhibit 6.1, we total the number of FTEs in each program. When you divide this by the total number of FTEs in the organization, less any FTEs in shared expenses, the result will give the percentage of people who work in the program and therefore the percentage of shared expenses that should be allocated to that program. As shown in our example in exhibit 6.1, the Rivers for All business line of Water Quality Monitoring would receive 25 percent of all shared expenses since 25 percent of all employees work in this program.

◆ ◆ ◆

Exhibit 6.2 Sample Personnel Costs

Rivers for All

Salary Split

Position	Annual Salary	Mission-Specific Programs				Fund Development Programs					
		Water Quality Monitoring	Training & Education	Community Engagement	Advocacy	Unrestricted Foundations	Membership	Events	Admin.	Shared	Total
Executive Director	90,000	4,500	9,000	9,000	13,500	11,700	10,800	9,000	22,500	–	90,000
Program Director	78,000	3,900	15,600	15,600	39,000	–	–	–	3,900	–	78,000
Finance Director	27,000	–	–	–	–	–	–	–	27,000	–	27,000
Outreach Coordinator	38,000	–	7,600	13,300	–	1,900	5,700	3,800	5,700	–	38,000
Water Quality Specialist	54,000	32,400	16,200	–	5,400	–	–	–	–	–	54,000
Water Quality Specialist	58,000	29,000	29,000	–	–	–	–	–	–	–	58,000
Water Quality Specialist	63,000	31,500	–	–	31,500	–	–	–	–	–	63,000
Development Coordinator	19,000	–	–	–	–	12,350	950	4,750	950	–	19,000
Total	427,000	101,300	77,400	37,900	89,400	25,950	17,450	17,550	60,050	–	427,000

We've now categorized expenses into the appropriate mission-specific and fund development program, split personnel expenses into each program using the staffing plan, and allocated shared costs using a FTE cost allocation basis. The last step to determining the true costs of each program is to allocate administrative expenses.

TEMPLATE 6.2   SALARY PLAN

Employee/Position	Salary	Mission-Specific Programs				Fund Development Programs		Shared Costs	Admin.	Total Time
		1	2	3	4	5	6			
Total Payroll Expense										

Administrative Allocation

Both audited financial statements and IRS Form 990 that nonprofits file annually list administrative expenses as separate standalone amount. For the matrix map, however, we allocate these expenses to each of the mission-specific and fund development programs that work toward accomplishing the organization's impact and financial viability. By definition, administrative expenses are necessary to keep the organization functioning and legal. They represent the time spent with the board of directors, keeping books and records up-to-date, and working with auditors. None of these activities are designed to generate revenue, but rather are obligations of being a corporation. Furthermore, while a strong administrative department might lead to an effective and efficient organization, it is hard to measure the mission impact of administrative activities by themselves. Does a good accounting system that produces meaningful financial statements lead to greater mission impact? On its own no, but by enabling strong management of other programs, it certainly does.

For these reasons, we do not create a separate program for administration, but rather split out the administrative expense among the other mission-specific and fund development programs. In doing so, we reflect that those programs are able to achieve greater impact with a strong administrative department and must also generate sufficient revenue to cover the organization's necessary administration. This is a similar approach that for-profit companies employ when they build the cost of their administrative functions into the pricing of their products and services.

There are many different methods by which an organization can allocate administrative expenses. We believe the easiest way is through direct expenses. The formula to calculate the percentage of expenses that each mission-specific and fund development program would receive is:

$$\text{Administrative expense allocation} = \frac{\text{Program expenses}}{(\text{Total expenses} - \text{administrative expenses})}$$

Taken together, the direct expenses, the shared expenses and the allocated administrative expenses we can now determine the true costs of each mission specific and fund development program and the total cost of running of our organization. Exhibit 6.3 shows fully allocated expenses for Rivers For All.

Allocating Revenue

The other component in determining profitability is revenue. Most finance staff are used to the process of allocating expenses, but allocating revenue to programs is not done in preparing financial statements nor the IRS Form 990.

Exhibit 6.3 Calculating True Costs

Rivers for All

Determining Profitability

	Budget	Mission-Specific Programs				Fund Development Programs			Admin.	Shared	Total
		Water Quality Monitoring	Training & Education	Community Engagement	Advocacy	Unrestricted Foundations	Membership	Events			
Expenses											
Personnel Expenses											
Salaries	427,000	101,300	77,400	37,900	89,400	25,950	17,450	17,550	60,050	–	427,000
Payroll taxes	32,666	8,227	6,291	3,146	6,049	1,657	1,367	1,270	4,658	–	32,666
Health insurance	16,000	4,030	3,081	1,541	2,963	812	670	622	2,281		16,000
Unemployment	7,480	1,884	1,441	720	1,385	380	313	291	1,067		7,480
Operating Expenses											
Project Expense	35,000		7,500	25,000	2,500						35,000
Travel/Mileage expense	3,500		1,000	800	800	100	300	300	200		3,500
Awards & recognition	500		150	200	150						500
Credit card and bank fees	900								900		900
Depreciation expense	2,000									2,000	2,000
Dues / Subscription Fees	1,500									1,500	1,500
Equipment	7,500		2,500	2,500	2,500						7,500
Events expense	3,000			500			500	2,000			3,000
Insurance	3,500									3,500	3,500
Licenses & permits	500				250				250		500
Meetings expense	3,800		1,000	1,000	500		800		500		3,800
Training / Conference	3,000		1,000	500	1,000		500				3,000

(continued)

Exhibit 6.3 *(Continued)*

Rivers for All

Determining Profitability

	Budget	Mission-Specific Programs				Fund Development Programs					
		Water Quality Monitoring	Training & Education	Community Engagement	Advocacy	Unrestricted Foundations	Membership	Events	Admin.	Shared	Total
Postage & delivery	3,250		700	600	350		1,000	500	100		3,250
Printing & reproduction	5,500		1,500	1,500	500		1,500	500			5,500
Accounting services	12,000								12,000		12,000
Consulting services	7,500		7,500								7,500
Rent	18,000									18,000	18,000
Boat expenses	3,500	3,500									3,500
Supplies	8,500									8,500	8,500
Total Expenses	606,096	118,940	111,063	75,907	108,347	28,899	24,400	23,033	82,006	33,500	606,096
Shared Allocation %	0	25%	19%	10%	19%	5%	4%	4%	14%	−100%	
Shared Allocation	0	8,437	6,452	3,226	6,204	1,700	1,402	1,303	4,777	(33,500)	–
Direct & Shared Expenses		127,377	117,515	79,133	114,551	30,599	25,802	24,336	86,783	–	606,096
Administration Allocation %		25%	23%	15%	22%	6%	5%	5%	−100%		
Administration Allocation		21,286	19,638	13,224	19,143	5,113	4,312	4,067	(86,783)		
Fully Allocated Expenses	606,096	148,664	137,153	92,356	133,694	35,712	30,114	28,403	–	–	606,096

To determine revenue allocation, go through each revenue stream and both mission-specific and fund development programs and ask the following questions:

+ *Does the program directly generate the revenue by charging a fee for service or other means?* If the answer is yes, the revenue that is generated by the program should

OVERCOMING THE CHALLENGE: WHICH NUMBERS DO WE USE?

The timing of the matrix map may not coincide perfectly with your fiscal year and it is hard to know which numbers to use: budget or actual. You want the matrix map to be as accurate a representation as possible of your organization's operations, and actual numbers tend to be easier for this, because budgets can be overly optimistic. However, if you use actual numbers, make sure that you exclude any large, nonrecurring, or one-time expenses. There is nothing wrong with using a budget, but ask yourself how optimistic the numbers are before you choose to use them. You should also use twelve months' worth of financial statements. While most organizations incur expenses evenly throughout the year, since payroll is paid routinely, revenues tend to be more cyclical because they correspond to foundation deadlines, appeals, or special events on the calendar. Using twelve months of financial information will smooth out these cyclical patterns.

be counted as a revenue for that program and allocated to it. For example, fees charged for pet adoption would be allocated to the pet adoption mission-specific program, whereas fees earned by renting your facility would be allocated to the facility rental fund development program.

* *If the program went away, would the organization still receive the revenue?* This question primarily refers to either restricted revenue or government contracts. If an organization receives foundation grants restricted to a particular mission-specific program, the revenue would be allocated to the program for which it is restricted. Likewise, revenue earned from government contracts

Exhibit 6.4 Sample Revenue Allocation

		Mission-Specific Programs				Fund Development Programs					
	Budget	Water Quality Monitoring	Training & Education	Community Engagement	Advocacy	Unrestricted Foundations	Membership	Events	Admin.	Shared	Total
Revenues											
Release from Restriction	35,950	–	10,500	10,450	15,000	–	–	–	–	–	35,950
Corporate contributions	95,000	–	15,000	80,000	–	–	–	–	–	–	95,000
Foundation contributions	184,725	29,725	25,000	40,000	65,000	25,000	–	–			184,725
Government contributions	75,000	45,000	17,500	12,500	–	–	–	–	–		75,000
Individual contributions	140,000	–	–	–	–	–	140,000		–		140,000
Membership / Program / Events	63,000	–	–	–	–	–	23,000	40,000	–		63,000
Miscellaneous	6,250	–	–	–	–	–	6,250	–	–		6,250
Interest	1,000	–	–	–	–	–	–	–	1,000		1,000
Total Income	600,925	74,725	68,000	142,950	80,000	25,000	169,250	40,000	1,000		600,925

would count toward the mission-specific program that generates it. This question is more subjective than the other, but use your best judgment when answering.

An example of the revenue allocation can be seen in exhibit 6.4 and template can be found at template 6.3.

TEMPLATE 6.3   REVENUE ALLOCATION

		Mission-Specific Programs				Fund Development Programs		Shared Costs	Admin.	Total
Revenue	Budget	1	2	3	4	5	6			
Total Revenue										

OVERCOMING CHALLENGES

Multiyear and Restricted Grants

Temporarily restricted and multiyear grants can distort income statements due to accounting policies. For purposes of the matrix map, we use unrestricted revenue, earned revenue, and revenue released from restriction for determining profitability. Therefore, for multiyear grants, use only the revenue and expenses associated with the current year, and for restricted grants, use only the revenue that has been earned or released. This will provide a clearer snapshot of the organization's operational sustainability. Having temporarily restricted net assets on the balance sheets provides the organization with the time and cushion to enact any changes necessary to its business model.

Allocating Fundraising Revenue

Allocating revenue among the different fund development programs is typically a straightforward process, with restricted revenue going toward a particular mission-specific program and unrestricted revenue split between the fund development programs. One common trap is thinking too hard about what category or program a donor "belongs" in. For example, a donor may be a major donor but give through a direct mail campaign. Which program gets credited with the revenue? While it is easy to overthink these seemingly important dilemmas, remember that you are ultimately trying to look at all the programs together and no one gift is going to make a significant difference on any program. Make your best judgment about which program ultimately received the donor's gift and allocate the revenue toward that program.

IS GUESSING GOOD ENOUGH?

Most people think that accounting is black and white: you put your accounts where they belong and in the end you have a balanced financial statement. Unfortunately, the reality is more about navigating shades of gray. Accountants want financial statements to be as accurate as possible. The issue in doing this analysis is to decide when enough is enough. The profitability numbers for your matrix map will not be audited and therefore don't have to be 100 percent correct. Think of this exercise more as an impressionistic painting than an actual picture: as long as the image reflects the reality of the situation you will be fine.

Challenges and Variations

In-Kind Donations

Every night a shelter for runaway and homeless youth serves over twenty-five youth, who often have been on the streets for days. When they come in, they are offered a shower, a hot meal, and clean clothes. The organization could never afford to pay for the food and clothing, but it is provided as a generous in-kind gift to the agency from a local restaurant and community members. The impact of these donations might be reflected in the mission impact score through building community, but these types of in-kind contributions are also vital to the financial success of community-based nonprofits.

In the world of accounting, in-kind donations net to zero as both an income line and expense category. For purposes of the matrix map, they should be included in the gross expenses for programs. Although they will be offset with in-kind revenue in determining profitability, the gross expenses are used to establish the bubble size on the matrix map. Including them in the expenses will demonstrate the true resources, both financial and in-kind, required to create the resulting impact.

Another option to showcase the importance of in-kind expenses is to alter the color of the program's bubble. As we'll discuss in more detail in the next chapter, bubbles are shaded based on the primary purpose of the program: mission specific or fund development. Other variations can be used, however, to show the percentage of in-kind contributions that go to supporting a specific program.

Volunteer Management

Similar to in-kind expenses if it weren't for the generous time of volunteers, many nonprofit organizations wouldn't be able to survive, yet alone thrive. Their impact on the mission is shown among the mission impact criteria, especially if building community around the organization or mission is used as one of the mission impact criteria. However, the presence of volunteers can also be shown within financial profitability. One method is to treat volunteers as we did with in-kind donations—by assigning a financial value to the work they are performing and having the resulting larger expenses demonstrated by the size of the bubble.

For example, a legal aid society relies on the pro bono time of local attorneys. It has one staff attorney who is paid a salary of $60,000. After taking into account payroll taxes and benefits, the full cost for this employee was $72,000, or $34.62 an hour. After calculating the hourly rate, legal aid staff determined the total number of volunteer hours they had in a year (6,500) and multiplied the two to come up with the value of volunteer services: $34.62 × 6,500 = $225,030). By adding the financial equivalent of the volunteer time together with the staff attorney's salary, the matrix map, through the size of the bubble, provides a much clearer picture of the resources necessary to accomplish the impact.

Many organizations that rely heavily on volunteers know that they don't just come in the door ready to help. Rather, they often need to be recruited, trained, cultivated, and recognized for their work. While the return on investment in volunteer management can be huge, it does require investment. For some organizations, this takes the form of a volunteer management department. In this case, volunteer management tends to be its own program with the profitability determined in the traditional way as a mix of direct, shared, and administrative costs.

Sometimes despite all the data, it is hard to monetize the value of volunteers. In this case, instead of risking the quality of the financial data, make sure you take into account the value of volunteers solely in the impact criteria.

Leading the Process

Just as assessing mission impact can be a new experience for senior managers, so too can the process of looking at mission-specific and fund development programs from a profitability perspective. The matrix map is an opportunity to build the financial literacy of both your board and staff by teaching them about the different types of expenses and cost allocation as we've outlined in this chapter.

As you build financial literacy, remind board and staff that profitability is only one of the two bottom lines in which we are interested. It is common for leaders of programs that are losing money to feel that somehow their program isn't as important or isn't doing well. On the contrary, their program may be the highest-impact program in the organization and a crucial component of a thriving, sustainable organization. Leaders should remind participants not to cast judgment early and not to be discouraged with the results. This valuable information will be considered together and equally with a program's mission impact before determining which strategy will create a more sustainable organization.

Templates

Go to www.nonprofitsustainability.org for online access to the following templates from this chapter:

+ Staffing Plan: Splits staff time among the organization's programs
+ Salary Plan: Used with the staffing plan, can be used to calculate personnel costs as well as determine cost allocation percentages by FTEs
+ Revenue Allocation: A template to split revenue by program

Summary

Determining the profitability of your programs may easily be performed by finance staff, but there are many key decisions that need to be made, and this is an excellent opportunity to raise the level of financial literacy among board and staff. Determine the true costs of each mission-specific and fund development program by allocating direct, shared, and administrative costs to each program. A staffing plan that reflects where staff are spending their time may be helpful to allocate personnel costs. Offset the total expenses with the revenue that each program is responsible for generating to determine the profitability. Remember that not everything needs to be profitable, but all expenses and revenues should be split among the mission-specific and fund development programs.

Creating Your Map

There's folklore in many cultures of several blind men each touching a different part of an elephant to discover what it is like. Different stories and arguments emerge among the men as they get together to describe the object they felt. The man who felt the tusk reports the object is hard like a stone, while another reports it is soft and flexible after feeling the trunk. While each story is vital, no piece of information on its own projects the sheer majesty and power of the whole elephant. Only when we put them all together can we see the elephant.

For the three previous chapters we've been the blind men, focusing on individual aspects of the organization: intended impact, programs, mission impact of programs, and profitability. Each of these is an important aspect of the organization overall, but until we put them together, we can't understand the power and sustainability of the organization. This is the next step in the matrix map process (figure 7.1).

While there is much to be learned from the individual steps of assessing impact and determining profitability, the true power behind the matrix map comes from putting all the pieces together to see the complete picture. In this chapter, we explore how to create the visual matrix map and share some tips on how to make it legible and meaningful for users. We also provide examples of variations of the map that may be useful to your organization and discuss the best way to present the map to your board.

Figure 7.1 The Matrix Map Process: Picture Your Map

Like many other aspects of this process, there are multiple ways to approach putting your map together. This chapter focuses on using a spreadsheet or graphing program to create your matrix map and then showcasing it to staff. You can also create a map using flip charts as part of a facilitated meeting. We cover this process in more depth in the boxes, as well as in the next chapter on analyzing your matrix map. Regardless of the process you use to put the map together, the finished product is composed of the same parts.

Creating Your Matrix Map

To create your matrix map, we start with two axes to graph impact and profitability. Profitability is graphed on the horizontal or *x*-axis. Mission-specific and fund development programs are placed on the axis according to their profitability determined in chapter 6, with the break-even point being in the middle of the axis. Programs to the right generate a surplus, and those to the left are not able to cover their full costs.

Impact is graphed on the vertical or *y*-axis, with impact increasing the higher it is placed on the axis. Unlike number lines that start at 0, the bottom of this axis is 1. When we assess mission impact, we rate programs on a scale of 1 to 4. The result is that the lowest score given is a 1, not a 0, and therefore 1 is at the bottom of the axis. This axis crosses the horizontal axis at 2.5, the halfway point of our impact score. The resulting graph, as shown in figure 7.2, creates four quadrants in which all the programs are placed.

Once the grid is in place, you can plot your mission-specific and fund development programs by drawing a circle for each program based on the mission impact assessment and profitability you determined previously. In this format, the map will show which programs are creating impact and how the organization is performing financially. A sample map is shown in figure 7.3. So readers don't have to guess at the financial condition revealed by the map, we also include a box that states the financial bottom line the map is demonstrating. The collective programs of the organization in figure 7.3 contribute to a $15,000 surplus.

After the circles are in place, you can shade them depending on their primary goal: mission-specific programs or fund development programs. In figure 7.3, the darker circles represent mission-specific programs and the lighter circles represent fund development programs. Although we treat all programs as equal, it is helpful to have the shading to understand the primary purpose of the programs. From an analysis perspective, which we discuss more thoroughly in the next two

High Mission Impact
Low Profitability

Impact →

Profitability →

High Mission Impact
High Profitability

Low Mission Impact
Low Profitability

Low Mission Impact
High Profitability

Figure 7.2 The Matrix Map

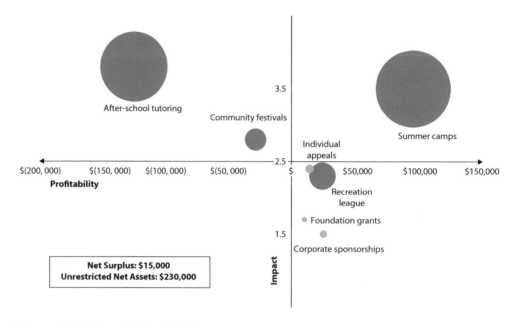

Figure 7.3 Sample Matrix Map

chapters, more questions are raised when a fund development program is losing money or a mission-specific program is low on impact.

The last step is to size the circles according to the total investment made in them. To do this, draw bigger circles for the programs with the highest gross expenses and decrease them in size until you reach the program with the lowest expenses. A program with total true costs (direct, shared, and administrative expenses) of $400,000 would have a circle twice as big as a program with total true costs of $200,000. By sizing the circles in this manner, you can tell with a quick glance at the map the organization's largest programs, how much is being invested in fund development programs, and the return on investment.

All of these steps will lead you to an image of your organization's business model. This will provide an explanation of how your mission-specific and fund development programs work together to create a sustainable organization that achieves impact and is financially viable.

Drawing Your Map Electronically

Since matrix maps were introduced, we've seen them in various styles from beautifully artistic renderings to impressionistic sketches on flip chart paper. If your artistic talents are more like ours (quite minimal), you can also create a matrix map on your computer using Microsoft Excel or another spreadsheet and graphing software package.

Mapping in Excel

The matrix map is created in Excel using the graphing function found under Insert in the menu. Under the list of charts or graphs, the matrix map is called a "Bubble Chart." Unfortunately, it is difficult to create bubble charts that treat each program as a new series of data. Therefore, we've created a template to use in creating your matrix map; you can find it at www.nonprofitsustainability.org.

The template will establish the basic structure of your matrix map, but you'll need to customize it for your organization. We'll discuss the basic structure here to familiarize you with the template and help you customize it.

There are three variables for setting up the matrix map: profitability, mission impact, and gross expenses. The first two drive where the program is plotted on the map, with the third variable, expenses, determining the size of the circle.

There are three variables for setting up the matrix map: profitability, mission impact, and gross expenses.

The first worksheet in the template is a table for data. It has four columns: the program name, profitability, mission impact, and expenses. Whether you are using the template or creating a matrix map on your own in Excel, set up the data in this manner. A complete table will look like table 7.1.

The template automatically generates the matrix map on a separate worksheet in the Excel file. The initial matrix map, which is for Community Senior Living, would look like figure 7.4.

Table 7.1 Data for Matrix Map			
Programs	Profitability	Mission Impact	Expenses
Senior housing	$120,000	2.8	$700,000
Resident services	(280,000)	3.9	1,600,000
Health fairs	(22,000)	3.8	473,000
Community outreach	(90,000)	2.4	110,000
Major donors	90,000	2.2	35,000
Foundation gifts	100,000	1.6	27,000
Direct mail	35,000	1.3	21,000
Special event	45,000	2.4	24,000

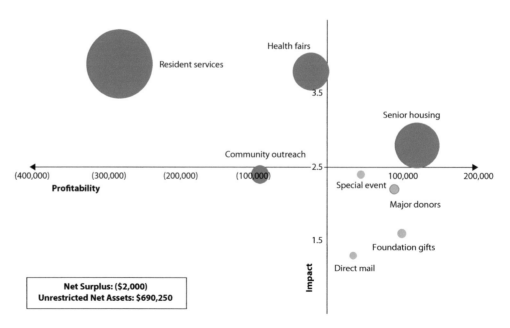

Figure 7.4 Matrix Map for Community Senior Living

Part of what makes the template different from simply using Excel's charting function is that it sets up different series, or groupings, for each program. This can be seen by going to Chart Tools on the menu bar and clicking on Select Data. The resulting table shows you each mission-specific and fund development program on the left and the corresponding data points. If you made your matrix map without the template, this is where you would go to add programs as series. The steps would be similar to our process for adding programs to our template.

ADDING MORE PROGRAMS THAN THE TEMPLATE ROOM HAS FOR

Adding programs is an easy step in the template:

1. Click on Chart Tools in the menu bar, and then Select Data. Alternatively, you can right-click on your map and click on Select Data when the menu pops up.
2. A dialogue box will pop up with each of your existing programs listed in the left-hand column under the heading Legend Entries (Series). Now say that you want to add another series. When you click on the button that reads Add, a new box will open, allowing you to define the new program. The variables to input are as follows:
   - Series name: This is the name of the program. Highlight the program name you wish to add back on your mapping data worksheet in column A and click Enter.
   - Series X value: The X coordinate is the Profitability variable found in column B on your mapping data worksheet.
   - Series Y value: The Y coordinate on the graph is the mission impact score, which can be found in column C on your mapping data worksheet.
   - Series bubble size: We're using the expenses for bubble size and they can be found in column D on your mapping data worksheet.

You can follow these steps and add as many programs as necessary to your matrix map.

Tip

The Quicker Map

Using the template for the matrix map will help shave some time off the process, but be sure to allow yourself enough time to make the matrix map legible. Technology, so helpful in many ways, can also add time, so if you really want to be quick, we recommend just drawing the matrix map with your task force. If your task force, board, or staff are already familiar with the matrix map, having a separate meeting to present the map may be unnecessary. If this is case or if you are time constrained in the process, present the matrix map, ask for initial feedback, and then move on to the analysis of the map.

Making Your Map Legible

We've all come to learn that the act of taking a picture is one thing, but using the computer to lighten it or make it more beautiful is a different art form. Creating your matrix map is no different. Once you have created the map, it may be beautiful to you, but creating a map that is legible and can be used and understood by your board and senior management is a different challenge. We're not going to actually change the picture, but rather augment it to make it easier to read. Here are some of the common questions that arise after a matrix map has been created electronically and ways to address them:

+ *How do I adjust the labels on my bubbles?* Sometimes the program labels have to be modified to work on the matrix map. Fortunately, they are relatively straightforward to change. In most spreadsheet or graphing programs, such as Microsoft Excel, the labels are actually text boxes. You can click in them and edit them right on the matrix map, including hitting Enter in the box if you want them to go onto two lines. To change the properties of the data label in Excel, right-click on the label and select Format Data Label on the resulting menu that pops up. From here, a dialogue box will appear, which allows you to modify many aspects of the label. Under the top category, Label Options, you can modify what the label tells you, changing it from business line name (Series Name) to profitability (X Value), mission impact assessment (Y Value), Expenses (Bubble Size), or any combination of these four. You can also change the position of the label to the left, right, above, or below the bubble. Another way to move the position of the label is to click on the box and drag it with your mouse, similar to how you would with a text box in a word processing program.

+ *How do I change the color on my bubbles?* Another common challenge with the matrix map is to get the colors right on the bubbles. You may use any color scheme that you choose, but we like to shade them based on their primary function—one shade for mission-specific program and another shade for fund development programs. We find that this is a helpful reminder to board and staff as they analyze the map that it represents all the activities of the organization and not just one or the other. Too often boards tend to focus solely on mission-specific programs and staff prefer them to focus solely on fund development programs, when in reality they need to focus on both. To change the colors of your programs in Excel, right-click on the bubble and click on Format Data Series. The menu that comes up has many options. If you go to the top option of Fill and select Solid Fill, an option will appear for you to change the color of the bubble.

  * *Why can't I see all the programs on my map?* For many organizations, one program is often much larger than the rest in terms of expenses. It may be the program the organization was founded for, or it could be the best-funded program. The challenge in the matrix map is that sometimes these programs overlap others and obscure them. One way to address this challenge is to change the order that the programs appear on the map. To do so, in the chart tools menu, click on Select Data or right-click on the map and click on Select Data. Overlapping programs are caused by the order of the programs in the mapping data worksheet. To change the order in which they are mapped, click on the larger bubble (the business line with the largest expenses) and move it toward the top of the list of the programs by clicking on the arrows side of the menu. Now the larger programs are mapped first, and the smaller ones appear on top of it. Of course, if the bubbles are the same color, they will still blend into each other. It is usually necessary to shade them slightly differently to differentiate the two programs.

  * *Everything is very close together. Is there a way to see them more easily?* One of the more common challenges that arise in the matrix map is that several programs will be grouped together, making it hard to discern any differences. This could be caused by any number of factors, but the first to consider is your process in assessing mission impact. In chapter 5, we addressed the task force's discussing the results of the mission impact assessment. Although there are certainly times when clusters of programs are appropriate, it may be an indicator of lack of candor in the assessment

process. As the task force reviews the mission impact scores, consider whether the score candidly and accurately reflects the impact of the mission-specific and fund development programs relative to the other programs. Remember that everything an organization does may have value, but not everything has the same value.

Clusters of programs may be appropriate for your organization. Organizations with long-established complementary programs often find that they have similar mission impact scores. Depending on the circumstances, however, small differences can be important. If, for example, an organization is financially stable with healthy reserves and running at a breakeven or surplus on its financial statements, any small difference between the mission impact score on the programs may be insignificant. However, if the organization is running a deficit and isn't financially viable, then the small differences become more significant in evaluating at which level to operate the program in moving forward.

One way to better visualize the small differences in your business model is to magnify the mission impact axis to highlight the differences.

One way to better visualize the small differences in your business model is to magnify the mission impact axis to highlight the differences. Take our example in figure 7.5. At normal scale in figure 7.5, there are multiple programs clustered around the 3.5 mission impact score. However, in figure 7.6, the scale of the *y*-axis is magnified to make the differentiation in the score more apparent. To magnify the map as shown in figure 7.6, you would:

1. Right click on the *y*-axis (the mission impact axis) and click on Format Axis.
2. In the dialogue box that opens, under the category of "Axis Options," there are options for the minimum and maximum of the axis. Normally Excel determines the amount automatically, but to magnify the map, you would manually adjust it by changing it from "automatic" to "fixed" and entering the minimum amount for the axis. In the example in figure 7.6, we change the minimum axis to 2.3.

Adjusting the axis magnifies the differences and makes the map easier to read. It is important to be upfront with potential users of your matrix map that the

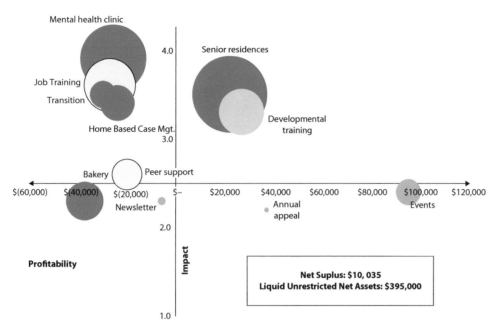

Figure 7.5 Magnified Matrix Map Sample—Normal Scale

map has been magnified. Otherwise, some might argue that it has been altered to express a particular point of view.

Drawing Your Map with Pen and Paper

While using a spreadsheet software to create your matrix map can be helpful, it can also easily be done with pen and paper in a facilitated consensual process. Here are the steps to do so:

+ Schedule a meeting with your task force and hang four pieces of flip chart paper on your wall in a 2-by-2 grid. Each sheet will represent one quadrant of the matrix map.

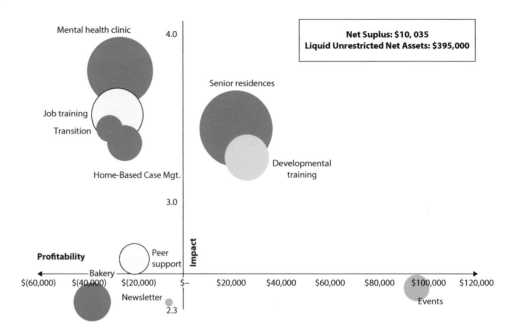

Figure 7.6 Magnified Matrix Map Sample—Magnified Scale

+ Where the left and right pages meet, draw a vertical line, label it "Impact," and insert a scale of 1 to 4. Where the top and bottom pages meet, add a horizontal line labeled "Profitability," along with the appropriate numbers based on your profitability analysis. The resulting image should be a matrix map like that in template 7.1.
+ Using a fifth piece of paper, cut out circles to represent each of the mission-specific and fund development programs you previously identified.
+ Place the programs on the quadrants based on the mission impact and profitability scores.

The physical act of placing the programs on the matrix map can be an enlightening moment for the task force and raise questions about the placement of certain

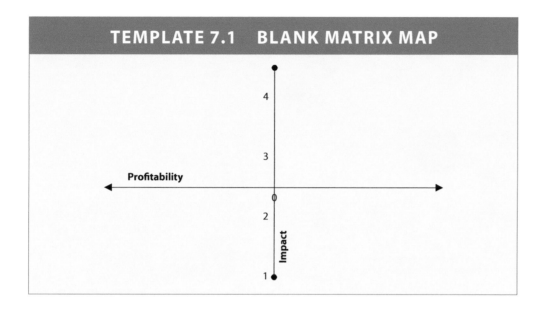

TEMPLATE 7.1   BLANK MATRIX MAP

programs. After you've completed the map, take a moment to absorb what you have completed and discuss the questions that it raises. If necessary, make adjustments by looking back at the mission impact criteria and the profitability calculation.

Variations on the Matrix Map

The matrix map as we've presented it in this chapter is designed to show the primary purpose of each program: mission-specific or fund development as determined by shade, as well as the profitability, mission impact, and general size (expenses) of each program. Some organizations want the matrix map to show other information, such as the number of people served or touched by a program or the history of a program. They accomplish this while maintaining the image of the dual bottom line by adjusting the color and or size of the program bubbles. For example, figure 7.7 represents the matrix map of an early childhood education

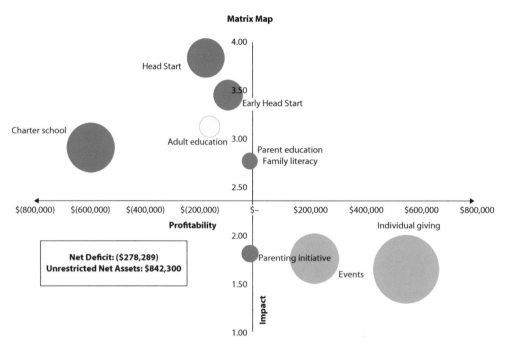

Figure 7.7 Matrix Map with Bubble Sizes Reflecting Number of Constituents Served

program. Over the course of the task force's discussion, it became clear that the number of youth served by the organization was a strategic issue and of utmost importance. Therefore, when they created their matrix map, they decided to have the bubble sizes of their programs reflect how many children they touch through that program. The resulting matrix map still showcases the organization's business model but also conveys this important information.

Another example of altering the size of the bubbles representing the programs is shown in figure 7.8. This organization had a history of rapid growth at various points in its history. As the task force grappled with their strategic issues, they

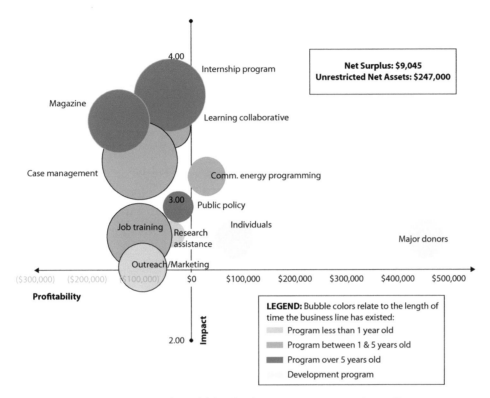

Figure 7.8 Matrix Map with Bubble Shading Representing Age of Program

wanted to know whether programs increased in impact and profitability the longer they existed or if their older programs performed worse as new ideas came along. Their solution was to shade the bubbles different colors depending on how long the program had been in existence.

Bubble color has also been used to reflect other variables, including volunteer engagement, number of in-kind donations that are a part of the expenses, and collaborations with other organizations.

These examples highlight the importance and flexibility of the map to reflect the needs of your organization. While maintaining the integrity of the map through the mission impact and profitability axes, adjusting the shading and circle size allows you to customize the map and make it more relevant to your organization.

Introducing the Matrix Map

With your matrix map now put together and legible, it is time to share it with others. Presenting the map to the task force or board and staff for the first time is an important moment. It provides an opportunity for them to engage with the organization in a new way and understand the organization's drivers for sustainability in a manner that wasn't as clear before.

Be prepared for a range of reactions from both board members and staff as you present the map.

Be prepared for a range of reactions from both board members and staff as you present the map. Board member reaction can range from confused to excited as they seek to first understand the map and then see the organization in a new way as the business model comes to light. Others may be underwhelmed. Board members who are well versed in the financial statements of the organization or the programmatic impact of the organization may see nothing new in the matrix map except a different way of presenting the same information. They may be seeking solutions, when the Matrix Map instead presents a path toward engaging decision makers in creating solutions.

Staff may share a similar reaction as well. They may initially overlook the organizational picture to focus solely on the performance of their program, seeing how it placed relative to others in the organization. Remind them as you present the matrix map to focus initially on the collective image of the programs. This provides you a more concrete sense of the organization's sustainability and can confirm or call into question intuitions about how the organization is performing. Then look beyond the picture as whole to better understand how each program contributes to overall impact and financial viability. Managers or board members more closely associated with programs of lower impact or profitability may get defensive or feel hurt.

The range of reactions can truly vary by organization and by the role and interests of people within it. It is leadership's role to remind people of the purpose of the matrix map and the process for getting to this stage. The map is not meant to be about the organization's shortcomings, but rather is a way to engage board and staff alike in the discussion of how to achieve exceptional impact in a financially viable manner. To begin this discussion, it is best to begin the analysis of the matrix map by looking at the complete picture. For that, we turn to the next chapter.

Template

Go to www.nonprofitsustainability.org for online access to the following template from this chapter:

+ Blank Matrix Map: A grid to start you off in drawing your own map

Summary

Creating and presenting the matrix map may seem almost anticlimactic after having worked to choose mission-specific and fund development programs, assess mission impact, and determine profitability, but it is the main event of the process and the beginning of the fun of understanding your business model and setting priorities to increase your organization's sustainability. Before you get to that, though, you want to make sure that the map is legible. There are many ways to create a matrix map, including drawing your own map, using a spreadsheet software program such as Microsoft Excel, or using a template available at www.nonprofitsustainability .org. Don't be afraid to customize the map for your organization, either zooming in on the axis to provide more differentiation between programs or even changing the significance of the shading of programs to convey different information. With your matrix map ready for presentation, begin by looking at the big picture.

There are many ways to create a matrix map, including drawing your own map, using a spreadsheet software program such as Microsoft Excel, or using a template available at www .nonprofitsustainability.org.

Reading the Matrix Map

Developing the Key Messages

I f this is the first time you are completing a matrix map or you haven't done one in a long time, it's likely that many people on staff and the board are digesting the organization's business model in this kind of holistic fashion for the first time. It is important not to jump to diagnosing specific program-level problems or opportunities before forming a higher-level narrative about the organization's overall business model and its implications for strategy refinement. This is a critical opportunity to finally have everyone in leadership—staff *and* board—truly understand the interplay of impact and economics in your organization. This widely shared understanding is still a rarity among community-based organizations, which has any number of negative consequences for the quality of staff decision making and board governance. Seize this opportunity to collectively digest the map (figure 8.1).

We advise that the task force develop three to five key points that together form the story the map tells about the organization's business model. For instance, a group might craft sentences like these:

+ Over the past ten years, we have successfully developed earned-income programs, but none of them is surplus generating when staff time is factored.

Figure 8.1   The Matrix Map Process: Analyzing Your Map

+   We have tried various things over the years to increase our support from individuals, but none of them has really broken through.
+   We have a break-even culture here: nothing loses too much money, but nothing makes much money either, so our balance sheet is very weak.
+   Our extensive use of volunteers and in-kind donations is essential to the health of our business model; we would be at risk if either faltered.

The idea is to capture the most important themes—the organizational truths, both flattering and potentially threatening, about how programs and money currently work together today.

Finding the Narrative: How Do Your Bubbles Cluster?

One way into your map's narrative is to explore why your bubbles cluster on the map the way they do. For instance, a common human services map is what we refer to as a *heart-money tree* (figure 8.2). These are often organizations whose direct

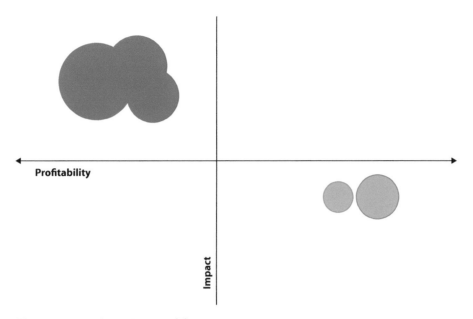

Figure 8.2 Heart-Money Tree

service programs are funded by government contracts that by design produce no financial margin. Thus, these organizations have multiple money tree programs to engage contributors. Without this philanthropic support, the government-funded services could not be sustained. It is possible to thrive with this model as long as leadership continues investing in the growth of the money tree programs and successfully advocates for and secures government funding. Assuming the costs to deliver on heart programs go up over time—higher salaries, higher lease costs, inflation, and so on—the fund development programs will have to meet or exceed that pace.

In this case, an example of a high-level theme could be: "Our government-funded programs are growing in expense and total net loss to our organization

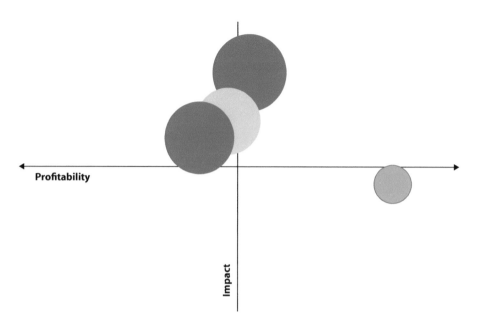

Profitability

Impact

Figure 8.3 Shining Star or Money Tree Matrix Map

faster than we are increasing the net return of our fund development programs."
Or perhaps you have most bubbles clustered along the middle axis—not making
much and not losing much money—and one significant star or money tree. We call
this *the shining star* or *money tree* business model (figure 8.3). For example, some
nonprofits essentially break even except for a major annual fundraising gala or a
successful program-related conference. Of course this will raise questions about the
organization's dependence on a single program for its financial viability. How is
the program's net return trending over the past three years? Do you have any
concerns about changing constituent needs or donor interests with respect to this
program? If you are uncomfortable with this concentrated dependence, how might
you create or shift a program to also generate significant net return?

In this case, an example of a high-level theme could be:

"We meet our budget each year on the back of one program, so we need to be
    continuously innovating that program to nurture its relevance and appeal
    to constituents and donors."

Many scrappy organizations, especially those led by vigilant budget moni-
tors, will have *y*-axis, *break-even* maps (figure 8.4). That is, nothing—including
their small-scale efforts at raising contributed income—is generating meaningful
surpluses. Grassroots and community arts organizations, for instance, often have
"*y*-axis" business models, with all of their programs lining up vertically along the
impact axis.

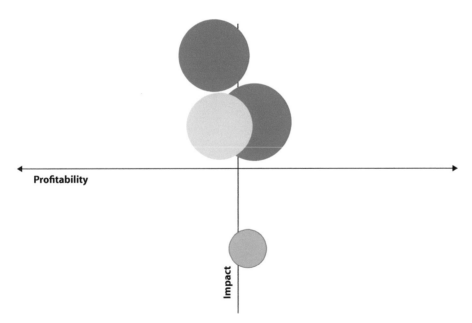

Figure 8.4 Break-Even Matrix Map

Such an organization might conclude:

"While we have been financially prudent in not spending what we don't have on an annual basis, we will never have our optimal theater space if we don't invest in our fundraising capacity and build a meaningful major donor program."

An organization whose bubbles all fall to the left of the *y*-axis is an organization in *crisis* (figure 8.5). From an organizational life cycle perspective, these are organizations that may need to consider closing or, instead, gearing up for a substantive reinvention. It is common for these organizations to have suffered unsuccessful leadership transitions or the emergence of new competitors for constituents and funding—or both.

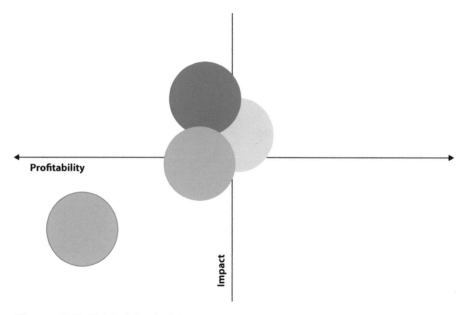

Figure 8.5 Crisis Matrix Map

Such an organization might conclude:

"We are unsustainable in our current form. Significant restructuring is our
    immediate priority."

A different, but equally unsettling, clustering of bubbles is the *stagnation* model
(figure 8.6), where everything falls to the right of the *y*-axis but is assessed as low
impact. This is an organization somehow realizing financial viability without delivering on its intended impact with excellence. This is a potential scenario when a
new leader steps into a traditional anchor organization in a community and realizes
that the impact framework has been absent; the mere need for services has justified
its existence. Through the rigorous application of impact criteria, the new leadership group can set the stage for badly needed innovation.

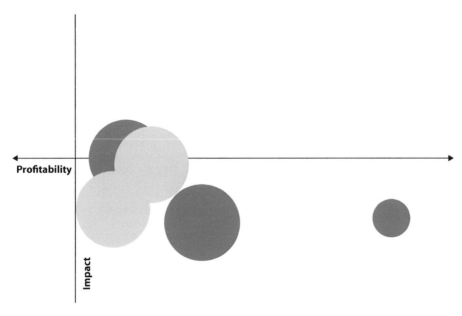

Figure 8.6 Stagnation Matrix Map

Such an organization might conclude:

> "We allowed our programs to stagnate over the last ten years and are fortunate to have the financial resources and new leadership capacity to begin innovating toward intended impact."

Healthy organizations are generally a mix of hearts, stars, and money trees, with the occasional stop sign that is addressed as quickly as is feasible.

There is not one generically optimal cluster of program bubbles. There are, of course, clear problem constellations: multiple, expensive stop signs, for instance, or the crisis and stagnation models. Healthy organizations are generally a mix of hearts, stars, and money trees, with the occasional stop sign that is addressed as quickly as is feasible.

Do You Have "Right Revenue"?

Another way to explore the narrative of your map is to assess the vitality and alignment of your major revenue strategies. In our practices, we often talk about this as "right revenue"—the state of your revenue working in concert with your intended impact and values. As we discussed in chapter 1, despite all kinds of advice pervading the nonprofit sector about income diversification, the fundamental question is this: Do you have the right revenue to pursue your intended impact in a financially viable manner that is aligned with your organizational values? Answering this question is an important part of creating the narrative for your map. To determine the qualities of right revenue, we suggest that your group look comprehensively at the revenue strategies manifest on your map and ask five questions.

Does the Current Revenue Mix Reliably Produce a Modest Surplus?

You may not have right revenue if, taken as a whole, it does not reliably produce a modest surplus for your organization annually. There is a difficult analysis here, though: potentially the revenue streams are capable of resourcing your intended impact with a modest surplus, but you have not yet invested in building the skills, systems, and culture needed for them to do so. (For instance, see the discussion on the culture of philanthropy in chapter 1.) In that case, it's not about abandoning a stream but achieving greater excellence in one or more of them. Relying entirely on government contracts and small, restricted grants is unlikely ever to produce a reliable surplus for an organization, so the combination of these two streams alone is rarely right revenue.

Interrogating whether your existing revenue streams could produce modest surplus annually may also include a discussion of increasing margin with current streams. In other words, are there viable ways you could increase the return of one or more streams without significantly increasing expenses on a relative basis over time? This would typically be through raising prices for fee-for-service programs, event tickets sales, or in proposals and contracts with foundations, corporations, and government agencies. For instance, have you been committing to too much service for the available dollars—doing more with less as so many nonprofits have done since the Great Recession—with institutional funders? Can you work proactively as each grant or contract is up for renewal, for instance, to reset expectations and get more of your full cost of delivery covered?

After exploring this question of the potential of your streams to produce modest annual surpluses, note whether you want to emphasize maximizing current streams or whether it's time to consider removing or adding a revenue strategy. Perhaps you might launch a major donor program to augment the annual campaign and government contracts or acknowledge that a special event whose net return continues to shrink while consuming more and more staff time has finally run its course.

Do We Have a Reliable Source of Unrestricted Support?

Unless your fee for service or restricted sources has been negotiated for a profit margin, a lack of reliable unrestricted income will lead to a lack of cash reserves and

A lack of renewable unrestricted cash can leave organizations completely at the whim of their institutional funding sources without sufficient capital to innovate.

serious financial constraint. A lack of renewable unrestricted cash can leave organizations completely at the whim of their institutional funding sources without sufficient capital to innovate. In many ways, this condition mitigates the presumed competitive advantage of community nonprofits over other institutions—seeing reality on the ground—because they cannot rapidly integrate that learning into new methods and practices. Unrestricted cash is also necessary for the practical reasons of managing cash flow variations, responding to emergencies, and weathering unexpected shifts in funding. Organizations that can get to the point where just 8 percent of their annual budget is in the form of renewable unrestricted income, for instance, will have a month's cash built into their business models.

Unrestricted income comes from one of three places: profit (net, *not* gross) on earned income strategies, unrestricted donations, and, for organizations with sizable endowments, interest earned. Here again we offer a caution about too much diversification in pursuit of that reliable 8 percent or more of unrestricted income. It's hard to do all of these strategies well. Which unrestricted income type best fits the core competencies of the organization and the profile of its core constituencies?

Are Our Largest Sources of Income Paying for Work That We Deem Essential to Our Intended Impact?

You may not have right revenue if your most significant funding sources are keeping the organization committed to delivering programs that have lost relevance or that won't allow the kind of innovation you believe is essential to deepening impact. Certain kinds of government funding, for instance, may constrain your approach to working with program participants in ways contrary to your emerging theory of change. In this case, your organization may be meeting half of the definition of *sustainability* (the financial half), but not meeting the mandate to develop, mature, and cycle out programs to be relevant to constituencies over time. Taking the second half of the sustainability definition deeply to heart may require leaders to walk away from funding streams that won't lead to this necessary dynamism in program design and innovation. Of course, making the strategic decision to move away from a historically significant funding stream is complicated and may require a slow, thoughtful exit to support clients, staff, and community members through a transition. In our experience, leaders who achieve staff and board focus on intended impact will regularly find themselves weighing the true value—not merely the dollar size—of each potential funding source: "Does it catalyze us toward impact or distract us with less important work?" Not all money is good money when your primary lens is intended impact.

Are We Relying on a Funding Stream That Is Changing Substantially, and Is That Change Beyond Our Control?

As government policy (e.g., the Affordable Care Act) and institutional giving strategies change (e.g., United Way's Campaign to Cut Poverty in Half by 2020), nonprofits may find that a stream they have long relied on is either going away or changing dramatically beyond their control. In other cases, the change is powerful but potentially influenceable; for example, the aging of the live theater audience means lower ticket sales unless and until nonprofit theaters figure out how to appeal to younger audiences. Reckoning with the severity and timing of such a change as early as possible is critical. If one of your key funding streams is changing dramatically or going away, how proactive should you be in changing your program models? Should you experiment with seeking a new kind of funding for the work currently paid for by a changing stream? Do you have the capacity to be successful in a different funding stream? What would that success require from board and staff immediately and on an ongoing basis?

Are We Relying on a Funding Stream That Is Misaligned with Our Organizational Values?

As organizations evolve, new leaders emerge, and the politics of philanthropy change, an organization might find itself in values misalignment with a particular funding source or a funding stream altogether. You do not have right revenue if board and staff feel a substantive dissonance with a funder's perspective on the work or the constituents being served with their resources. There is increasing recognition that nonprofits have brands too; taking resources from individuals and institutions with contrasting brands can hurt morale internally and raise suspicion among core constituents. Certain corporate donations and sponsorships may fall into this category, for instance. Or consider advocacy organizations working to pressure elected officials on current policy decisions; they may determine that taking government funding is out of alignment with their values, at least until they have seen the social change for which they are advocating. Or it may be something more internal to the organization, such as a museum deciding to make admission free seven days a week so that art and culture are democratized in alignment with their values.

There is increasing recognition that nonprofits have brands too; taking resources from individuals and institutions with contrasting brands can hurt morale internally and raise suspicion among core constituents.

Understanding "Right Revenue"

Answering these five questions in light of your matrix map may lead to one or more key parts of your map's high-level narrative—for example:

> "Renewable gifts from individuals are the best complement to our grants and contracts; we need to completely reimagine how we build a powerful culture of philanthropy at our organization to make them possible."
>
> "Our dues from members have declined consistently over the past three years. We need to determine if this is a dying or a salvageable revenue strategy for our organization."

"Even though we have been experiencing dissonance and conflict with some politically misaligned donors, our strategy of bipartisan community engagement requires that we maintain a big tent approach to fundraising."

Ideally, with revenue strategies, we want what Jim Collins called the "flywheel effect"—where what we care deeply about, what we can be best in the world at, and our resource engine are truly working in concert.[1] Getting to this right revenue and doing the ongoing work to stay there is integral to the sustainability mindset, and one of the very hardest parts of nonprofit leadership. For many groups, the matrix map process is their first time as a leadership team in questioning the alignment of their revenue streams with their long-term intended impact. Many organizations have grown organically with a "get programs paid for" mentality rather than a "get impacts paid for" mentality. The particular power of this process is in forcing the holistic discussion of impact and money. The resulting discussion may lead the organization to rethink its optimal revenue strategies and to set about intentionally shifting strategy over time.

Making a clear pie chart as shown in figure 8.7 of revenue strategies today and what your organization wants for three years from now can be a concrete touch point.

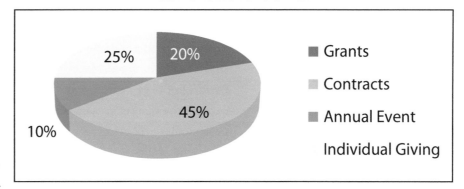

Current Revenue Mix

- Grants
- Contracts
- Annual Event
- Individual Giving

25% 20% 45% 10%

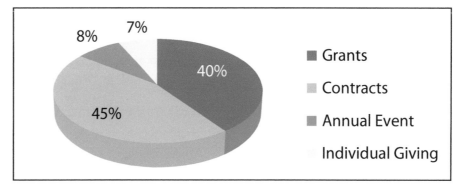

Desired Revenue Mix in Three Years

- Grants
- Contracts
- Annual Event
- Individual Giving

8% 7% 40% 45%

Figure 8.7 Revenue Mixes

Are the Dynamics of Our Market Landscape Changing in Critical Ways?

A third way into the high-level narrative of your map is to notice how much the changing dynamics of your market landscape have affected how participants assessed the impact or financial return of your programs. Many nonprofit fields are in states of disruption, with what constitutes impact being wholly rethought and new actors—sometimes from the for-profit sector—entering all the time. Programs that used to fill a critical gap in services may now be experiencing competition for participants, for instance. Programmatic approaches that used to be understood as best in class may now be perceived as behind the curve. Funding that used to be spread among many organizations may now be directed to a select handful of organizations, and so on. If this is the case, the task force will want to explore the market in which their nonprofit operates from three overlapping perspectives: collaborators and competitors, donors and funders, and clients and other stakeholders.

Our Position in Our Field or Movement

Nonprofit organizations collaborate and compete—and sometimes alternately with the same actors. None will achieve their intended impacts without the success of many other organizations too, so we have to be mindful of how what we offer complements or replicates what others with similar intended impacts are doing. Questions the task force might explore include these:

- What are the three to five most similar organizations to ours in our market or discipline?
- Are their programs growing or changing in ways that move them closer to or further from our approach and constituency?
- Have they developed programming that is superior in impact to ours?

There is great advantage in having the board and staff leadership up-to-date on these actors. First, it better prepares them to consider partnership opportunities with these actors. Second, it can give your organization a kind of permission to discontinue a financially unsustainable program knowing that another group can absorb your clients or constituents. And third, if you do view your programming as superior from an impact perspective, it can provide you with insights into how to communicate that distinction to funders and stakeholders.

Assessing your current matrix map through the lens of field positioning is more critical than ever before as the approaches to problem solving in communities and movements become increasingly integrative and holistic. This is a higher question than, "Are we competitive enough?" This is a question of our relevance beyond our four walls to our field or movement. We anticipate that insular leaders and organizations will lose ground quickly in the coming decade as the nonprofit sector activates networks and cross-sector collaborations to come at endemic challenges in new ways. Questions the task force might explore include these:

Assessing your current matrix map through the lens of field positioning is more critical than ever before as the approaches to problem solving in communities and movements become increasingly integrative and holistic.

+ Do others in our community or field seek us to be a partner?
+ Do we actively contribute to networks critical to our intended impact?
+ Do we have staff and board members viewed as thought leaders in our community or field?
+ Do we have strategic relationships in the government and business sectors?

Exploring your field positioning in light of your matrix map may lead to one or more key parts of your map's high-level narrative—for example:

"We are not leveraging existing partnerships with other safety net service providers in our community to meaningful effect. There is an opportunity for our leadership if we step up."

"Whereas our departed founder was viewed as the go-to voice on strategy in our movement, now stakeholders look to the leaders of other organizations to set direction. We've lost ground."

"Now that XYZ nonprofit has established such highly regarded programming for boys and young men of color, we are likely seeing the last of that funding this year ourselves unless we collaborate or innovate quickly."

Our Perception among Donors and Funders

A second and potentially overlapping lens on where your organization currently sits in your market landscape is how your donors and funders perceive your organization now. As you take in your matrix map as a whole, identify any important trends, positive or negative, that you see in the commitment of your key donors and funders to the organization. (The group will draw on its historical data and current experience in fundraising to have this conversation.) Of course, there is great diversity in the motivations of various donors and funders, so this is a nuanced analysis. Take each of your key segments and ask, "Does the snapshot of our matrix map reflect that segment's high and increasing commitment to us, a status quo commitment to us, or a waning commitment to us?" People and institutions invest for a combination of reasons: personal gratification for individuals, a critical need for services for government, fulfilling corporate social responsibility mandates for business, and advancing the progress of a community or movement for foundations for example. Depending on the segment, your clarity about intended impact and core strategies—and the regularity with which you have communicated them to these segments—may be an important factor in their current commitment levels. If the group senses important dynamism in how your work is being perceived by key investors, use template 8.1 to organize a conversation about it. Table 8.1 provides the beginning example of an analysis.

TEMPLATE 8.1   DONOR AND FUNDER COMMITMENT ANALYSIS

Donor/Funder Segment	Motivation	Perceived Commitment

Table 8.1 Sample Donor and Funder Commitment Analysis

Donor/Funder Segment	Motivation	Perceived Commitment
Major donors	A livable, vibrant community; personal satisfaction and recognition	High; we moved more annual donors to major donor status last year than any prior year
Foundations	Economic security for low-income community members	Medium and waning; increasingly our metrics do not impress program officers looking for programs that work.

Exploring the commitment levels of key donors and funder segments in light of your matrix map may lead to one or more key parts of your map's high-level narrative—for example:

> "We are making our case well to individual donors in our community, but institutional funders are looking for measurable results that we have not yet built the capacity to provide."
>
> "Local governments appear to be shifting their resources to larger nonprofits with higher capacity to manage contracts; we are perceived as low capacity from an infrastructure perspective."

Our Perception among Clients and Participants

Finally, explore the positioning and perception of your organization through the eyes of clients and participants. Did the assessment process surface any changes in how or which clients and participants are engaging with your organization? Did you assess waning scale, for instance, in program(s) that used to experience higher demand? Did your task force actively debate the depth of a historically signature program in light of clients' more current expectations of results? Are clients and participants choosing one or more of the other organizations you identified as sharing your market landscape? If so, why? Is your approach to community building still resonating with your community?

We regularly experience the matrix map interpretation process as bringing to light trends among clients and participants that only some people on the staff were seeing firsthand.

We regularly experience the matrix map interpretation process as bringing to light trends among clients and participants that only some people on the staff were seeing firsthand. Strategic decision making requires all of this information to surface systemwide. It may inspire further analysis through participant research (focus groups, surveys, interviews, and so on) to make meaning of the patterns emerging.

Exploring the changing perception and engagement of clients and participants in light of your matrix map may lead to one or more key parts of your map's high-level narrative—for example:

"Despite our more favorable reviews, audiences are increasing at XYZ Theater while we have seen a 10 percent drop in each of the previous two years."

"More and more volunteer organizers who have been through our three-month training are moving on before completing a full campaign cycle with us."

Developing Your Messages

Now that you have considered your completed assessment process and resulting map through the lenses of how your bubbles cluster on your map, the alignment of your core revenue strategies, and your positioning in a changing market landscape, distill the three to five key messages of your map. For instance, from the sample themes in this chapter, a community organizing nonprofit's task force might conclude:

Key Matrix Map Messages for a Community Organizing Organization

+ We meet our budget each year on the back of our statewide conference, so we need to be continuously innovating that program to nurture its relevance and appeal to attendees and sponsors. [*bubble cluster analysis*]
+ Our dues from members have declined consistently over the past three years. We need to determine if this is a dying or a salvageable revenue strategy for our organization. [*right revenue analysis*]

- Whereas our retired founder was viewed as the go-to voice on strategy in our movement, now stakeholders look to the leaders of other organizations to set direction. We've lost ground as thought leaders. [*market landscape analysis*]
- We are making our case well to individual donors in our movement, but institutional funders are looking for measurable results that we have not yet built the capacity to provide. [*market landscape analysis*]
- More and more volunteer organizers who have been through our three-month training are moving on before completing a full campaign cycle with us, limiting our return on our significant training investment. [*market landscape analysis*]

Understanding these core business model truths will ensure that when the task force moves to quadrant-by-quadrant analysis of the map and considers the trajectory of each individual program in the model, those considerations will be sensitive to these high-level realities.

These messages should be shared with all board and staff. Understanding these core business model truths will ensure that when the task force moves to quadrant-by-quadrant analysis of the map and considers the trajectory of each individual program in the model, those considerations will be sensitive to these high-level realities. This will help to prevent siloed or unrealistic decision making; all program-level decision making has to be in the context of the overall system's strengths and weaknesses.

Template 8.2 summarizes the key questions for the task force to ask when first reading their matrix map. Again, not all questions need to be asked, but these provide a guide on how to approach reading your map from a macrolevel perspective before looking at individual programs. Template 8.3 provides a worksheet to record your key messages and translate those into key priorities for the organization to improve its financial and programmatic sustainability. As you form the key messages from your map and the priorities that emerge to strengthen your sustainability, reflect back to the strategic issues you identified at the beginning of this process in chapter 3. The task force should consider if they are aligned. If not, they should consider whether their thinking has evolved through the mapping process or whether you're missing another message.

TEMPLATE 8.2   READING YOUR MAP

Questions for the task force's consideration:
How Do Our Bubbles Cluster?

- Heart or money tree
- Shining star
- Break-even
- Crisis
- Stagnation
- Other or mix
- What is the message behind how our bubbles cluster?

Do We Have the Right Revenue?

- Does the current revenue mix reliably produce a modest surplus?
- Do we have a reliable source of unrestricted support?
- Are our largest sources of income paying for work that we deem essential to our intended impact?
- Are we relying on a funding stream that is changing substantially, and is that change beyond our control?
- Are we relying on a funding stream that is misaligned with our organizational values?
- What is our desired revenue mix?

Are the Dynamics of Our Market Landscape Changing in Critical Ways?

Position in field or movement:

- What are the three to five organizations in the market most similar to ours?

- Are their programs growing or changing in ways that move them closer to or further from our approach and constituency?
- Have they developed programming that is superior in impact to ours?
- Are we a sought-out partner by others in our community or field?
- Do we actively contribute to networks critical to our intended impact?
- Do we have staff and board members viewed as thought leaders in our community or field?
- Do we have strategic relationships in the government and business sectors?

Perception among donors and funders:

- What is the motivation behind our key donors or funder segments?
- What is the perceived commitment of our donors and funder segments?
- What trends do we see in our support and revenue strategies?
- Should we complete a donor and funder commitment analysis?

Perception among clients and participants:

- Are there any changes in how or which clients and participants are engaging with our organization?
- Are clients and participants choosing one or more of the other organizations listed above over us?
- Are clients satisfied with our overall level of performance?

Creating a Business Model Statement

Whereas mission and intended impact are about what change you work to create in the world, the business model statement captures the fundamentals of what you do and how it drives your resource engine.

Once you have identified the high-level narrative of your matrix map, we recommend creating a business model statement—the dual-bottom-line complement to your intended impact statement (or existing mission statement). A business model statement describes your organization's revenue strategies and how they are linked to impact. This is yet another way—along with your key messages created above—to ensure that everyone is fully internalizing the economics at play in the organization. Whereas mission and intended impact are about what change you

---

TEMPLATE 8.3   MATRIX MAP MESSAGES

What are the key messages from your matrix map?

What are the top three to five priorities to improve your business model?

---

work to create in the world, the business model statement captures the fundamentals of what you do and how it drives your resource engine.

Here's an example of a possible business model statement for the community organizing group whose high-level map messages we listed above:

Business Model Statement for Community Organizing

> "XYZ engages the community in our organizing efforts through membership dues and an annual donor campaign, while our convening and advocacy work is supported through restricted grants from state and national foundations."

Notice how the business model statement does not focus on results but on the what and how and the accompanying resources they generate. Here are some more examples to get you thinking:

Business Model Statement for a Safety Net Service Provider

"XYZ leverages in-kind donations of food and medical services in its dining rooms and clinics and combines individual donations, major donor gifts, and unrestricted support from local foundations and corporations to provide comprehensive family case management."

Business Model Statement for a College Readiness Organization

"XYZ leverages corporate partnerships to secure qualified mentors and sponsorships from regionally headquartered companies invested in a prepared workforce for our state."

Template 8.4 can be used to record your business model statement. Often the task force may refer back to the impact and revenue strategies articulated for each program at the beginning of this process and discussed in chapter 3.

TEMPLATE 8.4 BUSINESS MODEL STATEMENT	
Programs	**Revenue Strategies**
•	•
•	•
•	•
•	•
Business model statement:	

Templates

Visit nonprofitsustainability.org for online access to the following templates in this chapter:

- Donor and Funder Commitment Analysis: Helps understand the motivation and perceived commitment of key donors and funders
- Reading Your Map: Captures the key questions to ask when initially looking at your map
- Matrix Map Messages: What are the top three messages your map is telling you?
- Business Model Statement: Describes your organization's revenue strategies and how they are linked to impact

Summary

This chapter is about spending the time necessary to derive the key organizational-level learnings that the process of holistically assessing impact and financial return surfaced. We walked through three potential lens of your map's key messages—how your bubbles cluster, the alignment of your revenue strategies, and your positioning in a changing market landscape—to develop three to five key messages. We also developed a business model statement to capture succinctly the fundamentals of what the organization does and how it generates resources. With these in hand, your task force is ready to turn to a quadrant-by-quadrant analysis and consider mission-specific and fund development programs for potential strategic decision making.

Program-Level Strategic Inquiry

Now, with a shared understanding of your matrix map's messages about the strength of your overall organizational business model, it is time to turn to a program-by-program strategic inquiry based on where on the map each of your programs lands. Your organization's performance is the aggregate performance of your programs, so continued rigor and candor in these conversations is critical. Over a series of task force conversations, consider each quadrant and inquire into why each mission-specific and fund development program landed there and what the group's thoughts are for initial decision-making implications.

For each quadrant (figure 9.1), we offer a simple starting point—a strategic direction for the group to consider and ultimately argue for or against with respect to each program that lands there. This is intended as a consistent way to start each programmatic conversation; you may ultimately decide differently. The key is to entertain options other than the status quo and to be in a stance of rigorous inquiry about the possibilities.

The Heart Quadrant

We'll start in the upper left and work our way around clockwise. The heart quadrant holds programs that you assessed as high impact but that on their own lose money (figure 9.2). If they are to be kept in the business model with their current

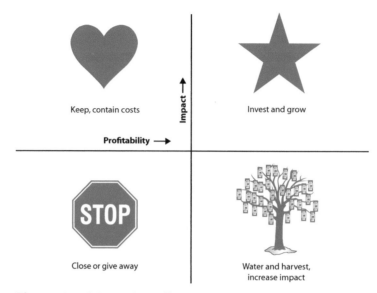

Figure 9.1 Matrix Map Strategic Direction Starting Points

Throughout this analysis, we stress the critical notion of financial interdependence: not everything has to generate a surplus, but the collective set of mission-specific and fund development programs must do so on a consistent basis.

income and expense structure, they will require continued surplus generation from elsewhere in the business model. That surplus can come from one of two places: the surplus generated by star programs or the surplus generated by money tree programs, or both. Throughout this analysis, we stress the critical notion of financial interdependence: not everything has to generate a surplus, but the collective set of mission-specific and fund development programs must do so on a consistent basis.

For heart programs, the strategic starting point is to keep and contain costs. We chose this because it is likely that you will be inclined to keep high-impact programs, yet you cannot allow them to cripple your organization financially. Therefore the first question is, "Can we envision this program achieving the same impact—or very close to it—with a different cost structure?" Most programs have a handful of cost-intensive elements—often salary, facility, and materials—so that's where you want to focus your inquiry. Is there a way to protect impact while changing the salary cost of the program? Might there be a different way of leveraging volunteers, including high-skill, professional volunteers such as doctors, therapists,

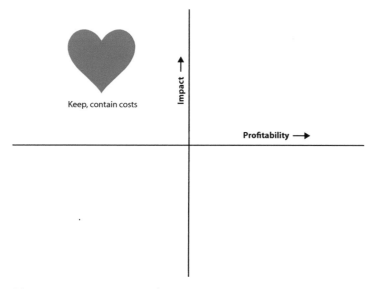

Figure 9.2 Heart Quadrant Starting Point

or retired teachers? Given the aging of professional baby boomers, this option may become a more viable one in the coming years.

Another tack on containing salary costs is increasing efficiency. Can a portion of what senior staff are doing be done by more junior staff? Can a better use of technology reduce the need for administrative staff? As uncomfortable as these considerations can be when potential jobs are on the line, it is essential to look at these factors. Again, the question always starts with the notion of protecting impact: Can a less expensive configuration of people potentially achieve the same impact? For other valid reasons, you may elect not to implement such options or to phase them in with staff attrition, but to leave them unexamined is not consistent with the sustainability mindset.

Facility is another cost that may be possible to approach differently without compromising impact. Technology allows more people to work remotely. Many public agencies have unused space and an interest in co-locating with nonprofits. Similarly, there may be different ways to think about the cost of critical program supplies; perhaps through in-kind support from for-profit companies. In sum, take a critical look at the nature of the relationship between large program expenses and the program's impact and consider potential alternatives. If there is anything expensive in the program model that does not drive impact, consider alternatives for it.

With heart programs, though, there may also be a different revenue strategy to consider. For instance, in human service organizations, heart programs are often core, government-funded services. It is worth considering whether a portion of your participants can pay a fee for their services while lower-income participants remain subsidized; we see this often in child care, education, and health care. More generally, organizations may elect to employ a sliding scale to ensure that those who can pay do so. In fee-for-service situations, testing to see if the market can bear a higher price—in the form of tuition, ticket sales, sale of goods, membership dues, participation fees, or something else—is critical. It is often the case that there is not a higher viable price or another renewable source of income given the economic profile of participants or the nature of the service, but it is worth the time to rule this out rather than assuming it.

If heart programs are ultimately deemed essential and have no surplus-generating possibilities, the group should be specific about the projected income needed to offset their losses over the near to midterm. Typically as your annual expenses for these programs increase, the losses will grow too. That means that the profit generated by star and money tree programs will need to keep pace. Often groups realize for the first time in this analysis that their fund development programs need to be in a very intentional growth mode to adequately sustain heart programs. *You can't decide to keep heart programs as is without determining where the profit growth in your business model is going to come from, including what investment of time and resources it will take to achieve that growth.*

As you conclude the analysis for each quadrant, note the potential program-level decisions that the group has surfaced. For the heart quadrant, examples might include these:

You can't decide to keep heart programs as is without determining where the profit growth in your business model is going to come from, including what investment of time and resources it will take to achieve that growth.

"As our current office lease approaches the option to extend, consider whether we can downsize to an administrative-only office and locate our youth programs on school and recreational center campuses."

"Others in our field make effective use of graduate-level interns. Conduct an analysis of potential cost-savings in our adult and family counseling programs."

The Star Quadrant

The star quadrant (figure 9.3) holds programs that you assessed as high impact and that on their own produce a surplus for the organization. These are relatively rare in the nonprofit sector. It's important to discern if a program is a star because

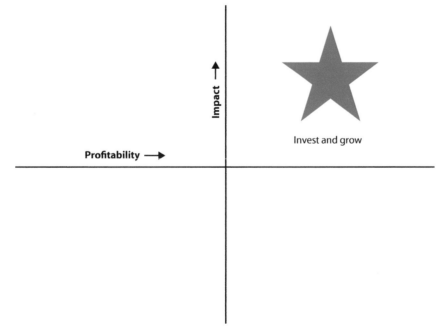

Figure 9.3 Star Quadrant Starting Point

of a nonrenewable infusion of income—we saw this during the recession with the American Recovery and Reinvestment Act funds, for instance—or whether there truly is a market-based margin built into the ongoing relationship between the program's costs and how you resource it. Assuming there is, the strategic starting point is to invest and grow. We chose this because the unfortunate tendency in too many organizations is to underinvest in star programs—taking them for granted and, in so doing, relegating them to eventual hearts.

A strategy of invest and grow requires first and foremost an understanding of why users or investors are both willing and able to pay above cost and staying much attuned to their needs and wants. This could be a government payer that has granted a fee for service that allows for a margin, in which case your leadership has to be engaged in ongoing advocacy for that funding stream and focused on achieving the measurable outputs and outcomes that government agencies typically expect in their contracting with nonprofits. If foundation funding is allowing for the margin, it may be especially important to understand the foundation's evolving theory of change—the larger community or social change it seeks and how you, in concert with its other key grantees, are contributing to that change. If the user is the primary payer, then understanding the price your user can afford, the value the user perceives, and the dynamic nature of your competition for its participation is essential. The idea here is for your staff and board leaders to have a deep understanding of the needs and motivations of the stakeholders who make your star programs possible. Furthermore, this understanding cannot be episodic as in the classic stakeholder interviews that happen every five years during traditional strategic planning; today, things change much too frequently for that approach. Instead, you need to be in an ongoing listening mode—dedicating meaningful staff, board, and volunteer time to learning what matters to your most critical users and investors.

The idea here is for your staff and board leaders to have a deep understanding of the needs and motivations of the stakeholders who make your star programs possible.

The strategy of invest and grow also means exploring whether there are opportunities to expand the program's impact—and thus your income from it. This could be through new geographies or new populations, or through developing complementary programming that draws on the core competencies and infrastructure of the existing program. Here too the idea is to protect, and indeed extend, the impact of the program. You are not looking for an investment that will achieve growth at the expense of current impact, only one that will deepen or extend the program's mission value. Investments might include hiring additional staff to meet growing demand, acquiring an additional facility to better serve a new community, or incorporating new technology for program delivery or evaluation purposes to support continuous innovation. Our caution to you is that you can safely add fixed costs like staffing and facility only if you feel confident that they will eventually contribute to the same revenue generation as the existing costs have—and at the same or a better surplus margin. Just as you want to extend impact by investing in and developing star programs, you also want to protect the precious surplus income that they generate. Star programs are not only critical in their own right; they help to make sustaining heart programs viable.

You are not looking for an investment that will achieve growth at the expense of current impact, only one that will deepen or extend the program's mission value.

As you conclude the star quadrant analysis, note the potential program-level decisions that the group has surfaced—for example:

> "Preliminary conversations with funders suggest there may be interest in our extending our early childhood education program to the adjacent county: we therefore must develop a business plan to understand the economics of expansion."
>
> "With only a modest investment of our time, the curricula we use in our teen pregnancy prevention program could be adopted for middle school students: we will meet with area principals to assess potential demand and pricing."

The Money Tree Quadrant

The money tree quadrant (figure 9.4) holds programs that you assessed as lower impact and that on their own produce a surplus for the organization. These are frequently fund development programs, but sometimes there are mission-specific programs that are profitable without having as strong an impact as other programs in the business model. The strategic starting point for these programs is to water and harvest in order to increase impact. From a financial interdependence perspective, the surplus these programs are generating is likely critical to the health of the business model overall. Certainly if the organization intends to sustain expensive heart programs, the growth of money tree programs is essential to sustainability.

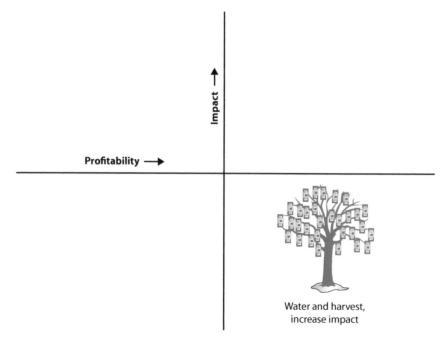

Figure 9.4 Money Tree Quadrant Starting Point

If the programs are for fund development, the strategic inquiry is focused on whether their net surplus can be increased, and if so, what investment that growth will require—a critical point. Usually it is not possible to increase the economic return of current fund development efforts without a meaningful investment—if not of cash, then of staff and volunteer time, but typically of both. For instance, if the organization is assessing the value of an annual special event, it may determine that increasing the corporate sponsorship for the event will require hiring an expert contractor on a seasonal basis each year. In this case, the analysis will be on the return on that investment over that time frame. Or it may be the profitability of the annual donor campaign that you intend to increase. In this case, you will need to factor in additional staff time, perhaps better technology, and the costs associated with stewarding more donors if you are successful in acquiring them.

While strategic investment is most typically the way to increase the scale and profitability of fund development programs, you also want to assess whether there are ways to reduce program costs and thus improve their margins. For instance, many organizations are moving away from hotel-based dinners to less expensive venues for their annual events. Many groups are making effective use of e-mail and social media–based fundraising campaigns to save money on paper, postage, and gift transaction administration. As with mission-specific programs, if there is a means of reducing costs without undermining the donor experience (or impact in this case), it should be employed so that margins go up.

It is also important to explore whether your fund development programs could achieve greater impact beyond their financial return. Part of having a true culture of philanthropy (see chapter 1) is recognizing the potential of these programs to be powerful engagement experiences for constituents—to inspire and educate them and in turn listen to them. Organizations that steward donors well ensure that fund development is relational, not transactional. Use the discussion of fund development money tree programs to identify ways to make each program a stronger platform for donor engagement in your cause or community. All donors—whether

Part of having a true culture of philanthropy is recognizing the potential of these programs to be powerful engagement experiences for constituents—to inspire and educate them and in turn listen to them.

they are individual community members, foundation program officers, or corporate social responsibility officers—are affected by meaningful interactions with your organization's most compelling stories.

In many cases, this involves assessing how well the fund development programs convey your intended impact and the values and principles that guide your pursuit of it. Sometimes fund development programs get stuck in the past—perhaps you have done an event in one way for twenty years or your newsletter has always been in a particular format—and need to be redesigned to match the organization's freshest thinking about itself and what matters most to its stakeholders. One way to think of this is brand alignment. In their recent book, *The Brand IDEA: Managing Nonprofit Brands with Integrity, Democracy, and Affinity*, Laidler-Kylander and Stenzel define *organizational brand* as "an intangible asset and identifier that imparts information and creates perceptions and emotions in its audiences."[1] Through this lens, you can think of fund development programs as having relatively more impact if they are intentionally and effectively imparting the most compelling information about who you are and creating the perceptions of—and emotions about—your organization and its work that will inspire donor engagement and retention.

What if you have money tree programs that are not fund development but rather mission-specific programs? This raises a different set of questions. For most groups, acknowledging that one of their mission-specific programs is significantly weaker or less relevant than others in their model feels different than discussing the impact of fund development efforts. They may ask, "Are we keeping this program solely for the surplus it generates? If so, are we willing to continue to invest in its capacity to generate this surplus?" or, "Are we comfortable with the opportunity cost of this decision; that is, deploying time and resources to this program that could perhaps be deployed on higher-impact programs to benefit our constituents?"

Perhaps the group is very comfortable sustaining the program as is. It plays a modest role in the organization's mission achievement but is an important financial contributor that can be sustained without undue burden on the rest of the system.

Or it may be that instead, staff are frustrated by sustaining the program. Maybe its weakness is apparent to outside stakeholders and thus tarnishes the brand. Or maybe staff feel they could increase the program's impact but recognize that that would require spending more money and thus eliminate the surplus. Because of financial interdependence, the group has to consider how it would replace the surplus if it increases the program's expenses or eliminates it altogether.

In general, leaders should be comfortable with the reality that programs contribute in relatively different ways to organizational impact. At any moment in an organization's life cycle, a rigorous assessment will find variation in impact. The strategic inquiry is about assessing if there are unacknowledged costs to sustaining lower-impact programs such as staff morale, constituent frustration, or brand undermining. For mission-specific money tree programs, the group should explore whether there are ways to increase impact without infringing on the surplus. Could the program be more effective with a different staff person to come up with innovations? Sometimes programs get stale because the people running them have lost their edge in the field or discipline. Could the program be more effective if you were more disciplined about client selection, focusing on the clients with whom you can be successful? There are any number of cost-neutral strategic decisions that could potentially move a money tree mission-specific program up closer to a star.

As you conclude the money tree quadrant analysis, note the potential program-level decisions that the group has surfaced—for example:

> "By putting a new cross-disciplinary team on our annual conference design, we're going to strengthen the content without undermining its important financial margin for us."
>
> "Compared to similar arts organizations in our community, our annual gala has a mediocre net financial return. We are going to create a board task force, with an ambitious task force chair, to start fundraising six months earlier than we have traditionally and budget for a $50,000 increase to its net surplus."

At any moment in an organization's life cycle, a rigorous assessment will find variation in impact.

The Stop Sign Quadrant

Stop sign programs are those you assessed as low impact and that on their own lose money. The strategic starting point is "close or give away" (figure 9.5). On paper at least, why would you direct your hard-earned surpluses from stars and money trees on a low-impact program? We chose this because the tendency is to want to resuscitate stop sign programs, especially if they are legacy programs that board members, key staff, or a handful of donors are deeply attached to. The challenge to leadership is to envision the organization without the program—that is, to imagine the benefits that removing the program would yield in terms of time to work on programs with stronger impact, a greater sense of strategic clarity and alignment, and potentially better service to constituents when a provider better positioned to be effective absorbs the work your organization steps away from. These can be

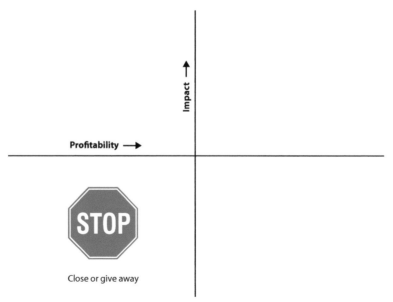

Figure 9.5 Stop Sign Quadrant Starting Point

challenging conversations, but if you can get people to articulate not just the loss that some will experience, but the benefits to the organization that will accrue, they can more easily pivot from fear to a courageous decision-making stance.

If, after considering closing or transferring the program to another organization, the group determines that to keep a stop sign in the model, begin with a thorough analysis of how and why the program landed in the quadrant in the first place. Are you using an outdated program model? Is the program improperly staffed? Have funders who historically supported the program turned away? In some cases, all three of these issues will be present at once; they are classic signs of a program that needs reinvention if it is stay in the portfolio.

Increasingly the nonprofit sector is adapting notions of innovation; in chapter 1, we noted the attention being put to "failing fast" rather than making big, expensive bets on long-term commitments or plans before you have had a chance to play—and fail—with an idea. The quote that's now ubiquitously used to drive this point home is one attributed to Thomas Edison: "If I find 10,000 ways something won't work, I haven't failed. I am not discouraged, because every wrong attempt discarded is often a step forward." We encourage you to take an innovation stance to programs that have lost their way. That might include engaging a cross-sectional team in your organization to spend two or three months unpacking the program's elements, paying sharp attention to the client or participant's experience and needs, and letting go entirely of the "this is how we have always done it" mindset. In fact, the "this is how we have always done it" mindset is very much at odds with the sustainability mindset.[2]

Of course, we cannot forget the economic impact of stop signs. The innovation approach assumes that the system can afford to direct funds to the program while the experimentation unfolds. For organizations without cash reserves or in financial crisis, this very well may not be the case. In this situation, closing the stop sign program—or perhaps "going dark" for a period of time—may be the best decision. This way you are not jeopardizing the financial health of the organization while you

The innovation approach assumes that the system can afford to direct funds to the program while the experimentation unfolds.

reimagine a program that is still potentially important to your intended impact. But in any scenario of keeping a stop sign in the model, we recommend a disciplined time line that is transparent to board and staff. How long will you give yourself to move this program out of the stop sign quadrant? What milestones of progress will you track along the way? And who will be involved in ultimately determining if you have succeeded—or instead need to let the program go?

As you conclude the stop sign quadrant analysis, note the potential program-level decisions that the group has surfaced—for example:

> "We are not ready to close our environmental education program in the schools, but it needs a complete reimagination. We are assigning a task force of two staff, two board members, and two community educators to learn about emerging practice and redesign the program. Their recommendation will be presented to staff and board in three months."
>
> "We need to close our workforce development program after twenty-five years of really valuable service to the community because we did not keep up with the methodological changes and funding streams. Other providers in our community are better positioned to serve our clients."

Process

There are several ways to go about the program-level strategic inquiry. One is for the task force to continue working together, exploring the questions outlined above and proposing program-level strategies back to staff and board leadership. Alternatively, you can open up the process more at this stage and engage a broader group, if not the entire staff, in program-by-program discussions. There are advantages and disadvantages to each, but generally we find that the best results come with an inclusive approach where program staff are engaged in developing the strategies that they will ultimately undertake. In larger organizations, the task force or a subset of it may engage departments or teams individually about a particular set of programs, aggregating these discussions as they go.

If you choose to engage a broader swath of the staff at this stage, it is very important to take the time to explain to them where you are in the process, share the matrix map with them, and convey the key messages developed from the organizational-level reading of the map before you get started on program-specific discussions. Just as it was with the impact assessment process, communication and transparency are critical to staff knowing how to engage effectively at this juncture and to their ultimate buy-in to the decisions ahead.

In addition to the matrix map and messages developed from the map (figure 9.6), template 9.1 summarizes the strategic questions that emerge for the programs depending on their placement on the map.

Understanding the strategic questions to ask for each program based on its placement in the map is an important first step. As you move through the questions and formulate strategies for the individual programs, template 9.2 will help capture

Figure 9.6 The Matrix Map Process: Analyzing Your Map

TEMPLATE 9.1   PROGRAM-LEVEL STRATEGIC QUESTIONS

Heart Quadrant

Starting point: Keep and contain costs

- Can we envision this program achieving the same impact, or very close to it, with a different cost structure?
- Is there a different revenue strategy to consider?

Star Quadrant

Starting point: Invest and grow

- Do we understand the needs and motivations of stakeholders who make the star possible?
- Are there opportunities (e.g., new geography, new population, complementary programming) to expand the program's impact and revenue?

Stop Sign Quadrant

Starting point: Close or give away

- Can we innovate this program to move out of this quadrant?
- How long will we give ourselves to move the stop sign?
- Is that the best use of resources?

Money Tree Quadrant

Starting point: Water and harvest, increase impact

- Can the net surplus be increased? If so, what investment will that growth require?
- Are there means to reducing the program's cost and improve the margin?
- Are there ways to achieve greater impact by making the program stronger?
- Is it aligned with our brand?

TEMPLATE 9.2   PROGRAM STRATEGY SHEET

Overview

Program Name:

Current Impact Assessment	Contribution to Intended Impact	Excellence in Execution	Criteria 3:	Criteria 4:	Current Mission Impact Score

Current Finances	Revenue	Expenses	Profitability

Current Matrix Map Quadrant:

Desired Matrix Map Quadrant:

◆ ◆ ◆

Strategy: Prioritized, with Most Important First

Strategy	Resources Needed	Implications on Impact/Finances	Priority: Organization or Program

◆ ◆ ◆

Is There Anything in this Program You will Stop Doing?		
Activity	**Implications**	**Resources Released**

the results of your discussions and the implications they may have on the organization's overall strategy.

The first half of the template serves to provide some context for the discussion highlighting the impact assessment breakdown and finances that resulted in the placement on the matrix map. These details help you ask questions such as, "Is our challenge with excellence in execution?" or, "Is our challenge more with our financial model, and is it generating as much revenue as it could?" Taken along with the market analysis and other factors discussed previously, the overview will help focus the conversation when formulating strategies to strengthen the programs.

The bottom half of the template allows a place for strategies to be listed, along with the resources needed to implement them successfully. We then ask you to consider the outcomes or implications the strategy will have for the program's placement on the map. Does this particular strategy focus on augmenting its impact, its financial strength, or both? Finally, we ask if and how the strategy relates to the organizational priorities that were developed when analyzing the map at the organizational level.

Templates

Go to www.nonprofitsustainability.org for online access to the following templates from this chapter:

+   Program-Level Strategic Questions: Summary of the strategic questions to be asked of each program
+   Program Strategy Sheet: Summary of the programmatic strategies moving forward to increase organizational sustainability.

Summary

In this chapter, we have walked you through the process of program-level assessment with a quadrant-by-quadrant discussion. Each quadrant has a strategic starting point to give the task force a disciplined way to start the conversation and ultimately find its way to the best possible decisions. Each program gets this level of review. With some, you will determine that no action is needed at this time, and with others, initial decisions that could be made in response to the program's quadrant location will emerge. We gave examples of these kinds of decisions throughout this chapter to stimulate your thinking. The objective is to leave this part of the process with a set of clear program-specific refinements and decisions that will become priorities for staff and board action and monitoring in the coming year.

Case Studies

Nonprofit organizations operate in different contexts. Their communities, funding sources, constituent needs, political environments, and desired outcomes are different. With all these differences, it seems a stretch to imagine that there is only one business model that will work for every organization. Yet too often processes focus on searching for the perfect business model outside the organization rather than building on the strengths right in front of us. The matrix map allows each organization to express its unique business model. Although many of these models are similar, the path to increasing sustainability differs based on where the nonprofit operates and what decisions the board and leadership are prepared to make.

In this chapter, we introduce you to several organizations that have used the matrix map to understand and strengthen their business models. We show some common challenges and solutions that resulted from the process as well as highlight each picture as a perfect business model in its own way, built on the organization's strengths and sustained by engaged leadership making strategic decisions that take into account both mission impact and financial viability.

Community Institute

Founded in 1983, the Community Institute works to sustain and build rural communities in the US Northeast. Its work is done directly with rural communities.

It is also a source of information through exchanging learning and experiences to further the sustainability of small, industry-related communities in the region and elsewhere. The organization was in the midst of an executive transition as the founder announced his retirement in the coming year, as well as the cyclical updating of its strategic plan when they started the process of creating a matrix map. Senior management hoped the map would help them better understand and assess their current programs and inform their strategic planning process.

To create the matrix map, the organization established a task force made up of the senior management team and led by the chief operating officer, who was slated to succeed the founder in the next year. This was a team of seven people: program managers, fund development professionals, and the chief financial officer. Because of the complex nature of this organization with its numerous programs, they decided not to include board members on the task force but rather have the task force report back to the board as part of their strategic planning.

The organization had an operating budget of $4.9 million with a surplus in the previous fiscal year of approximately $10,000. As is typical of nonprofit organizations, Community Institute found itself with some funding streams under pressure and new ideas that were emerging out of the planning process that were exciting but would require investment.

The task force identified two strategic issues at their introductory meeting. The first had to do with a sense of being overwhelmed that was felt among the senior management team related to the number of programs and initiatives that the organization operated. This was closely related to the second strategic issue, maintaining quality and maximizing impact while expanding. The organization had grown substantially over the past ten years, mostly by taking advantage of opportunities that came up and adding programs. The mission of sustaining and building rural communities allowed a broad set of initiatives, from encouraging civic engagement and education to community development. With an ever increasing broad range of programs and the board identifying several new initiatives during the strategic planning process, the task force was concerned about how programs were collectively working together to increase impact and whether the organization truly had the necessary skills on staff to deliver the programs in an exceptional manner.

The Matrix Map Process

The sense of being overwhelmed and the expansion were clear as the task force began identifying mission-specific and fund development programs. After listing everything the organization engages in, the task force identified twenty-seven such programs. No wonder they felt overwhelmed! An effort to consolidate them revealed that each program related to a separate initiative that the organization was undertaking. Furthermore, the discussion demonstrated that the programs were often thought of individually and not collectively. There was no easy way to consolidate them in one department. The task force truly saw the organization as twenty-seven different programs, each with its own identity. After double-checking with the finance staff that the organization could determine the profitability of all programs, it was determined to move forward and map them all.

The task force truly saw the organization as twenty-seven different programs, each with its own identity.

In selecting criteria to assess mission impact, the task force decided that they wanted a broad perspective and chose seven criteria:

+ *Contribution to intended impact:* How well does each program contribute to our intended impact of improving the quality of life in rural communities in the Northeast?
+ *Excellence in execution:* Is this program something our organization is able to implement in a superior or excellent way?
+ *Scale:* Does this program engage a significant percentage of people in the target community?
+ *Depth:* Does the program change the system to promote long-term sustainability, or is it an immediate solution?

+ *Competitive alternative:* Is this program the only one of its type being offered in the target community?
+ *Community and constituency building:* Does the program build community by engaging citizens in the target community?
+ *Leverage:* Is this program an entry into the organization? Do constituents come into the organization through this program and then move onto other programs—either fund development or mission-specific programs?

As you'll recall from the previous chapters, in our process we had said to choose only four criteria when assessing mission impact. The process of assessing mission impact is subjective, and adding more criteria will not make it any less so. We believe that focusing on the four most significant criteria for the strategic issues an organization is facing is a good discipline. However, sometimes a task force can get stuck selecting the four criteria and the strategic issues are broad enough that they are not helpful in prioritizing. This was the case with Community Institute.

Another concern with adding criteria is that it increases the number of questions in the assessment, especially if there are a lot of programs. For example, Community Institute had twenty-seven mission-specific and fund development programs, and each program would have to be assessed over seven criteria, which meant that would be 189 ($27 \times 7 = 189$) questions to answer. If they had narrowed the criteria to four, there would have been only 108 questions. The number of questions answered and the depth of knowledge required to perform the assessment was a consideration of the task force when deciding who should perform the assessment.

After much discussion, the task force decided on a survey pool of fifteen staff who had been with the organization for a fair amount of time and were deeply involved with the programs. They felt this pool (the task force members plus eight others) would possess the knowledge necessary. Because of the extent of the criteria and programs, the task force decided to use an e-survey for the assessment.

After the survey was set up, they held a meeting with all survey respondents to explain the process, the programs identified, and the criteria that were selected. Staff were given ten days to complete the survey and were allowed and encouraged to think over their responses and change them if they needed.

After the survey results were tallied, the entire survey pool got together to discuss them. Rather than progress program by program and criterion by criterion, the participants were provided the raw data ahead of time to think through any observations or scoring they wanted to talk about. The programs that saw the biggest range in scores (1 to 4 for example) were automatically discussed to see where the differences in opinion were. The discussion was deep and meaningful. It was, in fact, the first time this group had an intentional discussion around assessing the impact of their programs. There were discussions about the relative depth of programs and questions raised about whether some programs were truly scarce in the communities within which the organization works. All of these discussions informed and shaped opinions. After the meeting, participants had an opportunity to go back into the survey and make any adjustments to their scores they wanted to make.

Taking the revised score, the task force put together a matrix map. With twenty-seven mission-specific and fund development programs, it wasn't unforeseen that the first map had numerous programs clustered and was hard to read. (See figure 10.1.) To make the map more legible, they started by magnifying the impact axis and changing the bottom of the axis from one to two. No programs had fallen in the one to two range, so by changing the scale of the

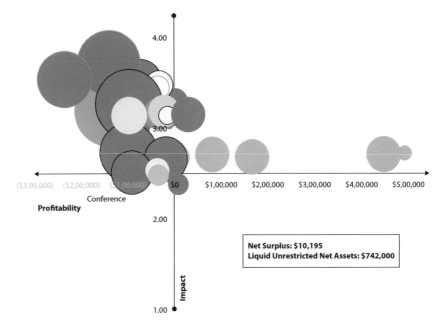

Figure 10.1   Initial Community Institute Matrix Map

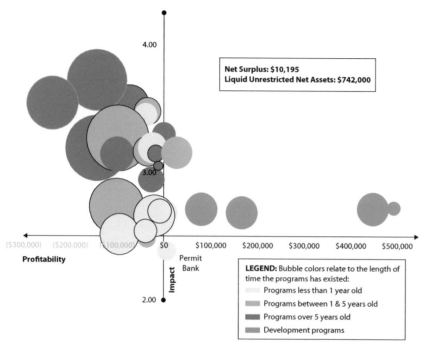

Net Surplus: $10,195
Liquid Unrestricted Net Assets: $742,000

4.00

3.00

2.00

($300,000) ($200,000) ($100,000) $0 $100,000 $200,000 $300,000 $400,000 $500,000

Profitability

Impact

Permit
Bank

LEGEND: Bubble colors relate to the length of
time the programs has existed:
- Programs less than 1 year old
- Programs between 1 & 5 years old
- Programs over 5 years old
- Development programs

Figure 10.2 Revised Community Institute Matrix Map

axis, they stretched out the programs and highlighted the differentiation between them.

The second change came out of the discussions the group had around the mission impact assessment. One of the issues that came up was whether older programs were having as much impact as newer initiatives or were being kept because of their historical significance. The task force thought this was an important strategic question and wanted to be able to visualize this on the matrix map. To do so, they used the age of each program to determine the shading of the bubble. Mission-specific programs that were over five years old were one shade, between one and five were another, and the newest programs (those less than a year old) were yet another shade. The resulting matrix map is shown in figure 10.2.

Analysis

While the revised map was more legible, anyone looking at the result could easily understand why senior management felt overwhelmed. After overcoming this sense, the analysis by senior management resulted in several observations:

- The shading of the mission-specific programs was effective in demonstrating that the older programs had more impact than the newer ones. There appeared to be a pattern of programs moving up the impact scale as they became more established. Initially the task force had felt that the newer programs might score higher because they held the promise of impact. The task force took the findings of these shadings in part as confirmation of the candor in their mission impact discussion.

* Their work in building an education and job training infrastructure in the communities they served tended to score higher on the impact scale than the policy and housing programs did. The task force looked back at the mission impact data once again to try to understand the reason for this. The data showed that the differences came primarily in excellence in execution and in leverage, meaning that people would come into those programs and then move on to others and that they were known for and good at developing education programs. These were important points to address in the strategic planning process.

* Like most other nonprofits, the organization relies heavily on unrestricted funding to be financially viable. The matrix map raised the importance of investing in fund development and ensuring a culture of philanthropy throughout the organization to continue to be sustainable.

Although the discrepancies among the mission-specific programs were small and none were necessarily in the stop sign quadrant, the task force took this information into the strategic planning process. Two programs were closed as a result of this process, and the matrix map provided the confirmation that a third, which was already in the process of being transferred to another organization, was on the right path. The task force took this step to focus on areas where they had strengths and to free up additional capital to develop even more expertise is those areas.

As the task force shared the matrix map with staff and the board, it created a shared understanding of how the organization's programs interacted. During the strategic planning process, the Community Institute explored new directions for some of its higher-impact mission-specific programs ensuring ways to maintain the high impact and used some of the savings generated from the closure of other programs to invest resources in higher-impact programs, fund development programs, and other new initiatives. In addition, the organization spent time understanding their theory of change and structure and reorganized their programs around five groups in which all the other programs now fall.

This case study shows the power of the matrix map in helping to organize a nonprofit from a chaotic listing of seemingly disparate programs to a comprehensible theme that the board, staff, and outside constituents can understand. Even with the large number of programs, it was still possible for the staff to come together and make suggestions about closing programs and investing in others. The matrix map also provided a firm understanding about where investment should be made and recommendations on where to free up capital for new initiatives, and it informed the strategic planning in a way that integrated the finances with impact resulting in a sustainable plan moving forward.

St. Elizabeth Housing

St. Elizabeth Housing is a faith-based nonprofit organization located in the Midwest that creates sustainable affordable housing solutions, primarily in its metropolitan region. It works toward the day when all residents, especially those economically disadvantaged, have a decent, affordable place to live and become part of a community. In its twenty-year history, the organization has sponsored, developed, or codeveloped over three thousand units of housing for low-income seniors and families. In addition to developing these affordable housing projects, the organization empowers local residents to achieve and sustain homeownership and financial success through counseling and assistance for first-time home buyers, people threatened by foreclosure on their homes, seniors interested in reverse mortgages, and lease-to-purchase residences. The organization also engages in property management and resident service programs, including home health care to allow residents to enjoy their residence and age in place for as long as possible.

Facing decreasing government funds and a changing business model, St. Elizabeth engaged in the matrix map process to better understand its current business model and make strategic decisions about its future. Not all the changes were negative; in fact, many opportunities were presenting themselves to the organization. Unfortunately, these opportunities arose on their own schedule, and most had not been foreseen during the previous strategic planning process. The senior management team and board wanted to increase their ability to adapt to a changing business environment by evaluating current mission-specific programs and new opportunities as they arose rather than once each year. As part of this process, in addition to the matrix map, the organization also engaged in a process of articulating its intended impact and theory of change to more easily communicate its goals and impact.

The Matrix Map Process

The task force members were the senior management team and the board chair, fund development committee chair, and treasurer. The task force had read the background on the integrated nature of the matrix map and nonprofit business models and came together ready to identify the strategic issues and name the mission-specific and fund development programs. The strategic issue that was named had to do with where the organization should focus. It was receiving interest in certain types of housing and losing funding in others. How should it best position itself to be able to accomplish its mission and remain financially viable?

The task force listed the programs in a fairly straightforward manner, but after discussion of strategic issues, it decided to split out mission-specific programs by the types of affordable housing that the organization built to better understand the impact and makeup of its efforts. The task force also discussed how to split the fund development activities into programs. The organization had not engaged in systematic fundraising efforts for unrestricted funds, so it was not used to thinking about fundraising in terms of programs. In reviewing their fund development efforts, they realized that most of their unrestricted funds came from individuals through their annual appeal. Therefore, they decided to add one program for these efforts. This resulted in eleven programs:

+ Real estate development for senior housing
+ Real estate development for lease-to-purchase housing
+ Real estate development for other housing
+ Foreclosure prevention
+ Homeownership services
+ Nonsenior property management
+ Senior property management
+ Resident services for lease-to-purchase homes
+ Resident services for senior buildings
+ Home health care
+ Individual fundraising

The task force engaged in much discussion around the mission impact assessment criteria and decided on four criteria that best aligned with St. Elizabeth's goals and mission:

+ *Contribution to intended impact*: In both absolute terms and relative to other programs, how much does this program contribute to the intended impact of the organization?
+ *Excellence in execution*: Is this program something that we execute in an exceptional manner?
+ *Scale or volume*: Does the organization serve a significant number of constituents with this business line, or does it have the ability to drastically increase its service where it can achieve reduced costs by economies of scale?
+ *Significant unmet need*: Are there alternate providers for specific business lines, and does the demand for each business line exceed the cumulative supply that St. Elizabeth and other providers offer?

Before the organization could use the contribution to intended impact criteria, the task force engaged in a process to better understand and articulate their intended impact. It is clear from the program list that housing development can imply many different things. St. Elizabeth had historically focused on senior housing, even starting a home health care program, but it also offered low-income housing and had engaged in efforts such as foreclosure prevention to help people remain in their homes. The discussion around intended impact went to the core of the organization and what it was trying to accomplish. The task force decided that although St. Elizabeth engages in lots of housing efforts, its target constituents were senior citizens living in their city. This didn't mean it wouldn't build other types of housing or build in other geographies, but senior housing in their community would be a primary focus and what it would hold itself accountable for. This was what had founded the organization and was once again clearly articulated as the intended impact of St. Elizabeth.

The discussion around intended impact went to the core of the organization and what it was trying to accomplish.

In addition to choosing the criteria, the task force decided to weight the business lines, recognizing that scale or volume might not be as important to them as the remaining three criteria and wanting to put extra weight on their choice of contribution to intended impact. To do so, when averaging the mission impact scores, the task force-weighted the criteria as follows:

+ Contribution to intended impact, 40 percent
+ Excellence in execution, 35 percent
+ Scale or volume, 10 percent
+ Significant unmet need, 15 percent

One of the goals in weighting the criteria was to show the importance of contribution to intended impact and excellence in execution over the sheer number of housing units developed.

After much discussion, the task force decided that they were best positioned to assess the mission impact. Each member of the task force was engaged deeply with the organization, and every program was represented. However, they wished to inform their assessment on more data. So the task force had the managers responsible for each of the eleven programs complete the program overview by providing basic information on program accomplishments, the number of people served, and the competition. The task force also researched other affordable housing providers to inform their impressions of excellence in execution and what it would mean to provide a high-quality service. With this information in hand, task force members completed the assessment on paper, assessing each of the programs on a scale of 1 to 4 on each of the four criteria. A meeting was then held to discuss the results.

At the mission impact assessment meeting, each participant discussed his or her scoring for the programs on each of the criteria. There was intense discussion about some of the ratings. One of the interesting observations was that board members were most familiar with the newer programs since they had more recently been discussed at the board level. At the conclusion of the meeting, the task force had assigned mission impact scores for each mission-specific and fund development program.

At the same time the impact assessment was ongoing, a subgroup of the task force began working on determining the profitability of the programs. The financial information provided a fair amount of detail, but the programmatic structure used for the matrix map was different from the financial statements the organization routinely prepared. The task force worked on segmenting revenue and expenses into the new mission-specific program structure and also focused on allocating administrative expenses among all the programs.

The task force subgroup met routinely with the full task force during the process to discuss the methodology of determining profitability and seek guidance and consensus as they proceeded. There was discussion about the administration allocation, as well as noncash transactions. The organization had some significant noncash transactions, including a noncash investment and depreciation on their financial statements. Most organizations keep depreciation expense when determining profitability and treat it as a shared expense that is allocated across all programs. However, for a housing developer, these costs can become quite significant. The task force decided not to include the noncash transactions (both depreciation and a noncash investment) because they would not add to a program's sustainability, thereby keeping the profitability on a cash basis.

Through the discussions of the task force around both mission impact and the discussion around profitability, St. Elizabeth provides a great example of developing staff through the matrix map process and creating shared understanding of the organization's financial and impact drivers.

The resulting matrix map for St. Elizabeth is in figure 10.3. The map showed a portfolio that is typical of many nonprofits with a wide range of impact and profitability among the organization's programs. The mix was not surprising to the task

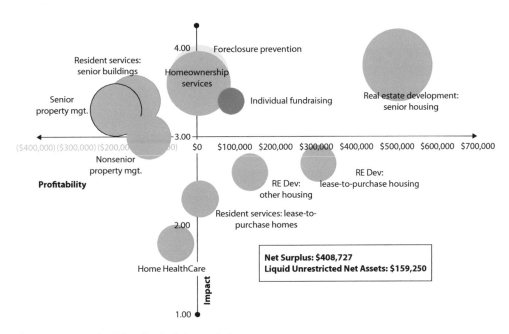

Figure 10.3 St. Elizabeth Matrix Map

force, and they were anxious to move on to the next step. The task force decided to break out each program, understand why it placed where it did on the matrix map, address the strategic questions raised for each program based on its placement on the map, and understand what it would take, in terms of both programmatic strategy and financial resources, to move the program. After doing this on an individual program level, the task force came back together to understand the implications for the organization overall and use the matrix map to make strategic decisions on how to increase the organization's sustainability. The decisions reached were as follows:

The task force reached out to other community developers and property managers to understand this field and learned ultimately that they didn't manage enough units to achieve economies of scale; moreover, it was unlikely that they would ever manage enough units to do so.

◆   *Property management*: One of the insights from the resulting matrix map was that senior property management was being subsidized at great cost even though it was a lower-impact program than some of the other mission-specific programs. In looking further into the mission impact assessment, the task force members realized it scored low because of their significant competition in that line of business and they were not as skilled at providing that service as they were with their other programs. The initial strategic direction for this program was to keep it but to contain costs. The task force reached out to other community developers and property managers to understand this field and learned ultimately that they didn't manage enough units to achieve economies of scale; moreover, it was unlikely that they would ever manage enough units to do so. During the course of their research, they discovered a property management firm with aligned values. Informed by their work on intended impact and theory of change and having looked at the matrix map, the task force decided to outsource this business line and reduce the subsidy. Nonsenior property management was a star for the organization. This was primarily because there were no other providers that did this service. While opportunities for this work are rare, the organization would continue to look for them.

- *Home health care*: This program was a stretch for St. Elizabeth from the beginning. It didn't quite fit in with their expertise in housing development, but it was an effective way to try and keep senior citizens in their homes. Home health care was administered through a partnership with another organization, and it was decided to outsource this program entirely to the partner, which is better equipped to manage this program.

- *Resident services*: Resident services is a growth area for St. Elizabeth. This area was a heart, aligned highly on impact. It was decided that with the resources generated from outsourcing property management, resident services would be reinvested with the hiring of a senior manager to oversee all activities.

- *Fundraising*: St. Elizabeth had not had a very formal fundraising program. However, given the environment the leaders find themselves in, they could use the unrestricted support to subsidize their work and build a reserve. The organization decided to invest resources to create a more robust fundraising system.

As part of the planning process, the organization completed a separate strategy sheet for each program describing the strategic direction from the matrix map, the current impact and financial strategies, and then the proposed impact and finance strategies. These sheets were then used to create goals and metrics to monitor progress. They also used these goals in their plan to project a future matrix map (figure 10.4).

The results of the matrix map and strategy process for St. Elizabeth dramatically reshaped the organization. It is now more focused on its impact, strengths, and how its programs interact to create a sustainable organization. The nonprofit has fewer staff and a lower budget due to the outsourcing. Some may say that the organization retrenched, but the staff feel more committed than ever before to the organization's mission with a shared understanding of what they want to achieve, how they will measure it, and how they will make it work financially.

Some may say that the organization retrenched, but the staff feel more committed than ever before to the organization's mission with a shared understanding of what they want to achieve, how they will measure it, and how they will make it work financially.

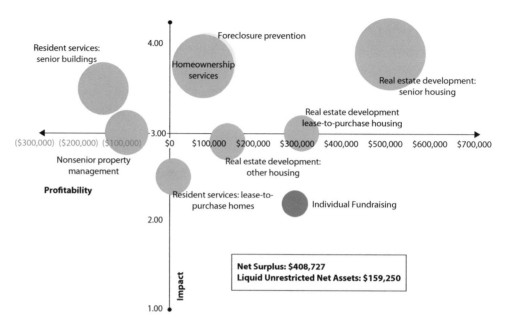

Figure 10.4 St. Elizabeth Prospective Matrix Map

Columbus Community Services

Columbus Community Services is a 114-year-old social service organization nestled in a small town in the US South. The organization has seen many iterations over its history, with its current mission focused on providing education and training to help its constituents find employment. While the current mission focuses on job placement, the organization has several programs left over from previous efforts, including a counseling program that was one of the initial programs of the organization and a swimming pool, which was included in the organization's building as an earned revenue strategy. While it might have seemed like a good idea at the time, the swimming pool had become a money pit. The executive director knew the organization was hurting its impact by continuing to fund these low-impact, non-mission-related programs. However, many of the people who used the pool were also on the board. Moreover, how, she wondered, could the organization get rid of its counseling program when that is what the organization was founded on?

With these strategic issues in mind, the executive director turned to the matrix map as a tool to engage the board in understanding the organization's business model in an inclusive way that looked at all the programs and the trade-offs of resource allocation. She put together a task force for the project made up of the senior management team and a couple of board members.

The task force's first meeting was spent becoming acquainted with each other, the theory behind the dual bottom line, and the matrix map process. The task force quickly agreed with the strategic issues that the executive director had identified and moved on to identifying the mission-specific and fund development programs. This is the list they came up with:

- English as a Second Language
- Adult literacy
- Job skills
- Counseling
- Computer center
- Special event luncheon
- Unrestricted foundation grants
- Individual donors
- Swimming pool

The task force met once again to determine the mission impact assessment criteria to be used. After much deliberation, they came up with the following four criteria:

- *Contribution to intended impact*: How much does this program, on its own and relative to our other programs, contribute to our intended impact of increasing the employability and employment of our constituents?

- *Excellence in execution*: Is this program something the agency does in an exceptional manner?
- *Competitive landscape*: If this program went away, is there a similar service that is offered in our community where our constituents could turn? The task force included this criterion because of the competition that the swimming pool faced. Part of the reason the swimming pool was losing money was that a city pool had recently opened up less than ten blocks away. The task force felt this would help focus the organization's resources where they were most needed.
- *Community building*: Does the program engage constituents with each other and help build a sense of community? Ultimately the community center wanted to build a vibrant community, both around the organization and within the city where they lived.

While the feeling was that the members in the room were best positioned to assess the programs, there was a legitimate concern that the board would not buy in to the results of the matrix map if they weren't part of the process of creating it.

With each of these criteria being important, the task force decided to weight each of them equally. The task force took time in answering the question of whom to survey. While the feeling was that the members in the room were best positioned to assess the programs, there was a legitimate concern that the board would not buy in to the results of the matrix map if they weren't part of the process of creating it. The decision was made to include the entire board in the survey pool, along with the senior management of the organization.

Since the organization wasn't in immediate financial trouble, the task force decided to roll out the survey in a deliberate manner. Their first step was to complete the program overview for each of the mission-specific and fund development programs that were being assessed. They then spent a special board meeting presenting the overviews so that board members had the same information for each program. Board members also had an opportunity to ask questions of the program managers. Board members were then told about the criteria and the process for the assessment.

Each board member completed the assessment right at the meeting on a sheet of paper. The scores were taken at that meeting and entered into to a spreadsheet so that everyone could see the scores and the average, which allowed for real-time analysis of the mission impact scores. Rather than going through each program and each criterion, presenting the scores on a screen overhead allowed board members to talk about whatever aspect of the assessment they wanted to. One board member brought up the range in responses on competitive landscape for counseling. The robust discussion that ensued resulted in the lowering of the score. This discussion continued for over an hour.

At the same time as the mission impact assessment was ongoing, the director of finance was working to pull together the profitability report. The organization's accounting system was set up by cost center, so it was easy to pull the information, with only the fund development programs needing to be separated.

With all the information present, the organization presented the matrix map in figure 10.5.

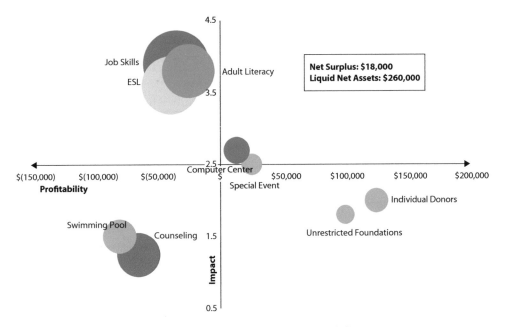

Figure 10.5 Columbus Community Services Matrix Map

Even after the mission impact discussion, the matrix map presented a new way for the board of directors to look at the organization. They knew that they were relying on unrestricted foundations and individuals to be sustainable, but they were surprised to see that both the swimming pool and counseling programs showed up in the lower-left quadrant.

Discussion eventually turned to how the organization could improve its counseling program. Of course, this is the fear with stop signs—the organization will spend more time and resources trying to resurrect a program than recognize the opportunity cost of using those resources to support its high-impact programs. The task force dug into why the counseling program scored so low on impact. It was rated high in contribution to intended impact but scored very low in excellence in execution and in competitive landscape. One board member summed it up by saying, "Counseling is important to the organization, but we're not very good at it and there are alternatives out there—presumably who are better!" As a result, the organization reached out to other organizations and formed a partnership with some of them. In this way, they were continuing to provide vital services to their constituents but were doing it in a manner that delivered superior impact and was financially viable.

One board member summed it up by saying, "Counseling is important to the organization, but we're not very good at it and there are alternatives out there—presumably who are better!"

The swimming pool was another point of contention. The conversation around the pool had always been done in isolation: "Should we keep the pool or close it?" In these arguments, board members who enjoyed using the pool fought vigorously to keep it open. However, even they knew that it wasn't the most important thing the organization did. When the matrix map put the swimming pool in the greater context of whether to keep the pool or invest in the job training program, the answer was clear, and the board voted to close the pool. Because the swimming pool had facility-related issues, the board first did further financial analysis to make sure they wouldn't lose more money by shutting down the pool than keeping it open.

Summary

Each of the case studies in this chapter presents ways of using the matrix map to make hard decisions. One was done as part of another strategic planning process, one was used as the strategic planning process, and one was used to bring the board along in making a decision that had lingered for too long. Each organization customized the process and matrix map to serve their needs and engaged different constituencies depending on the strategic issues they faced. While the matrix map process outlined in the book may appear to be linear and rigid, in reality the process is not. We hope these case studies give you freedom to take the process and make it work for the context in which you find your organization.

Bringing it All Together

The Tools and Processes of the Sustainability Mindset

Over the course of the matrix map process, you have created or refreshed six essential work products in support of organizational sustainability. Both the creation and maintenance of these interrelated elements foster the sustainability mindset across the staff and board. When you have completed the process, take the time to ensure that everyone in the organization understands what happened, what they learned through the process, and how to use the six elements in their day-to-day work or board service. In this final chapter, we offer some guidance and perspective on how the work you have done can stick and how to leverage it in spreading and strengthening the sustainability mindset across your organization (figure 11.1).

We begin with a review of how to name and position the value of each of the six matrix map process elements:

1. *Intended impact statement* (chapter 4). The most transformational thing any leader can do with her staff and board is help them shift from a programs-and-services mental model to an impact mental model. When we are focused on

Figure 11.1   The Matrix Map Process: Making Strategic Decisions

The most transformational thing any leader can do with her staff and board is help them shift from a programs-and-services mental model to an impact mental model. When we are focused on impact, we hold on loosely to any given program or methodology and instead have a continuous learning stance toward what's actually working now.

impact, we hold on loosely to any given program or methodology and instead have a continuous learning stance toward what's actually working now. When people are attached to programs and methods, the change to an impact orientation can certainly be daunting, but over time, empowering people to adjust and refine what they are doing through an impact lens makes the work enormously more gratifying, not to mention with strong impact. Your intended impact statement can and should change as your understanding of the issue and what's needed changes over time. The idea that nonprofit missions are timeless has held the sector back from innovation. Your intended impact statement can be one sentence. In our experience, it may very well replace your mission statement.

2. *Matrix map* (chapter 2). The matrix map, as outlined in this book, provides a powerful, one-page snapshot of how individual programs and the organization overall are progressing with respect to intended impact and whether that progress is financially viable. We see your most recent matrix map as a critical strategic document that should be at hand for all staff and board's reference.

3. *Business model statement* (chapter 8). The business model statement is the dual-bottom-line complement to your statement of intended impact. It succinctly

communicates the economic fundamentals of the organization—the primary resources (e.g., revenue types, in-kind goods, and volunteerism) that enable the organization's core strategies. Ideally these resources represent what we have described as right revenue, meaning that the resources are in alignment with what the organization wants to accomplish and with its values.

4. *Organizational strategies* (chapter 8). Strategies are not programs. They are the distinctive approaches you take to the work; they are the overarching choices you make in the delivery of your mission-specific and fund development programs. They are the approaches that amount in large part to your organizational brand or identity. For instance, "meaningfully connecting people of all faiths" is a strategy. One year an organization might express that strategy through an all-faiths community forum on reducing gang violence; another year it might express it through an all-faiths holiday giving drive, and so on. If it's a core organizational strategy, leadership will look for ways to express it in most, if not all, of its programs, and it will serve as a screen for which opportunities to embrace and which to reject. Typically an organization will have five to seven core strategies, each of which can be captured in a single sentence.

Strategies are not programs. They are the distinctive approaches you take to the work; they are the overarching choices you make in the delivery of your mission-specific and fund development programs.

5. *Organizational priorities* (chapter 8). Through conducting the matrix map process and thoughtful, inclusive annual planning—which is what we encourage—leadership will always have a handful of critical priorities. The kinds of messages you developed as you interpreted your matrix map may lead to these priorities. They may have to do with strengthening your business model, developing a critical capacity, or initiating a new program. All staff and board should be apprised of what these organization-wide priorities are—and engaged in setting them to the extent possible—so that they can contribute from wherever they sit to their achievement. Typically an organization will have three to five organizational priorities at any given time. For instance, "Establish a planned giving program" is an organizational priority, as are "Rearticulate the strategic value of the board of directors and recruit five new members aligned to that new articulation" and

"Expand programming into a new geography." We recommend articulating each priority in a compelling sentence or two and identifying who the steward is for the priority—that is, the person, team, or committee that will take the lead on ensuring that progress is being made and communicated throughout the life of the priority. Priorities should be constantly visible: post them on the wall in the staff room and boardroom; organize the executive director's monthly report to the board around them; ask people to share success stories along the way at staff and board meetings. People often say that what gets measured gets done, but we think it's as much about the stories and progress-sharing that happen.

6. *Program objectives* (chapter 9). Each time you complete the matrix map process, specific program-level objectives will emerge. They may also emerge as staff make sense of ongoing evaluation data or in the annual planning process. These are the mission-specific or fund development program refinements you plan to make in the near term to increase the impact or financial return of a given program. For instance, "Revise evaluation tools for the teen case management program" is a program objective, as is "Create campaign involvement screening process" to determine in which advocacy campaigns to engage. While program objectives will be carried out largely by a given program's staff and key volunteers, to ensure ongoing strategic alignment system-wide, all program objectives should be explicitly tied to intended impact and core organizational strategies.

Strategic People, Not Strategic Plans

In our experience, the sustainability mindset is nurtured less by lengthy strategic plans and more by keeping strategy front and center all the time. Figure 11.2 offers a framework for integrating the matrix map and other strategic elements into the everyday operations of nonprofits.

Indeed, working with the matrix map with our clients and incorporating and adapting the great thinking of so many practitioners as described in chapter 1 has

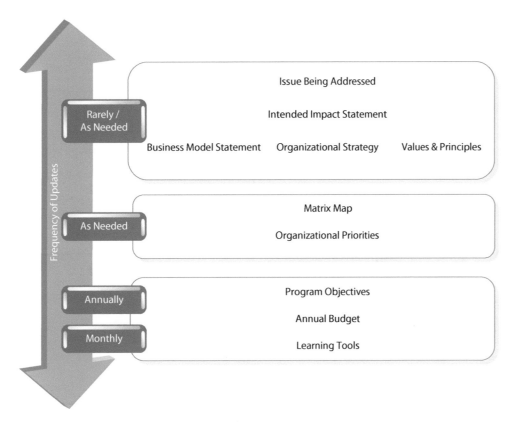

Figure 11.2 The Strategy Framework

led us to this different framework for aligning an entire organization around strategy. We are now partnering with our clients to capture the impact and strategy essentials on a single page as illustrated in figure 11.3, especially emphasizing the conceptual linkages among them. As a sector, we need to stop complaining about strategic plans that sit on a shelf and instead stop producing them.

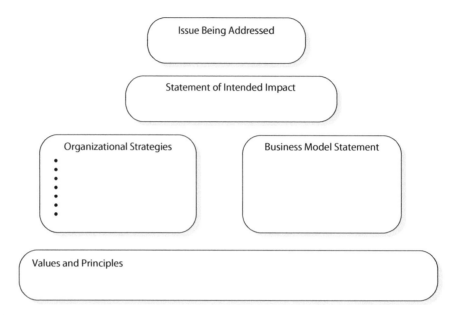

Figure 11.3 Organizational Strategy

When we complement this one-page visual with the organizational priorities and program objectives described in this book, we have, in just three pages, the critical articulations of strategy and direction for reference by all staff and board.

There are two essential, ongoing processes that further activate the sustainability mindset when they are done thoughtfully and inclusively: budgeting and evaluation. The annual budget is the financial expression of your core strategies, organizational priorities, and program objectives. Budgeting is really a form of program planning, and that's how staff and board should be engaged in it. Creating the organizational budget is the ultimate dual-bottom-line exercise. When budget building and monitoring is inclusive and explicitly tied to strategy, it nurtures the sustainability mindset across staff and board.

The "decision-making, execution, learning" cycle requires what Jim Collins called "the rigorous accumulation of evidence."[1] Given your intended impact, what evidence will you accumulate? For most organizations, this is not necessarily about proving causality without a shadow of a doubt (unless your work calls for that), but far more about continuous learning. What indicators of progress are most important to us? What data collected by others will we learn from too? How will we take in and act on evidence? What realistic systems and formats can we employ to engage all staff and board in meaningful learning? The answers to these questions will depend on your intended impact, capacity, and organizational culture, among other factors. But you must answer them. The evidence of what's working will inspire your staff to keep innovating, provide the ingredients of strong ambassadorship for your board, and assure your donors and investors that they are part of something real and important.

Cultivating the Sustainability Mindset

The six tools and concepts of the matrix map process are integral to the sustainability mindset, which in our view is a nonnegotiable leadership mindset for executive directors and board chairs. Our responsibility as leaders is to steward our organizations to deep impact in a financially viable way. But the real opportunity is in seeing leadership as a process, not merely a position, and looking for, cultivating, and celebrating the sustainability mindset in all staff and board. We know that leadership can and does occur anywhere in a system—be that system a team, an organization, a network, or a movement. Thus, the more people holding the sustainability mindset across the system, the more likely that system will be continuously capable of making strong, dual-bottom-line decisions that drive impact and financial health.

Indeed, the core competency of the sustainability mindset is decision making. In both our previous book and this one, we have argued against our sector's tendency to prioritize planning to the neglect of bold, transparent decision making.

But the real opportunity is in seeing leadership as a process, not merely a position, and looking for, cultivating, and celebrating the sustainability mindset in all staff and board.

As consultants ourselves, we often feel in executives' request for strategic planning an unconscious request for collusion in deferred decision making. So how do we reconcile a deep conviction that shared leadership is superior to the leadership-from-the-top model with a preference for the seemingly centralized act of decision making over the traditionally inclusive process of planning? We do it by embracing inclusive decision making.

One of the most powerful aspects of the matrix map process is the engagement of a cross-section of board and staff in frank, organizational self-reflection. Our experience is that in so doing, you won't be able to put the proverbial cat back in the bag. Now, more people, and maybe all of them, understand the business model and its implications enough to participate effectively in future decisions. Now all of the strategic nuance is not living solely with the executive director and one or two of her or his colleagues. And at the same time, the executive director has a deeper understanding of the work from the perspectives of people across the organization; his or her thinking will be changed and broadened by this process too. Now more people are primed to participate in the "decision-making, execution, learning" cycle at the heart of year-round, strategic behavior (figure 11.4).

Throughout this book, we have emphasized inclusivity and transparency. This doesn't mean that every staff and board member is involved is all aspects of the matrix map process or of strategy formation more generally, but it does mean that everyone is clear on how key processes will unfold. And it also means that everyone is supported in interpreting and applying the learning and refined strategies in their own work or governance. Similarly, by inclusive decision making, we don't mean that everyone is involved in every decision, but rather that nobody makes important decisions alone. Decision points become explicit opportunities to activate strategy. Even if an executive director has proportionately more influence on a given decision, it is in her and the organization's best interest to engage others in weighing the options against core strategies. Three good things happen: various perspectives

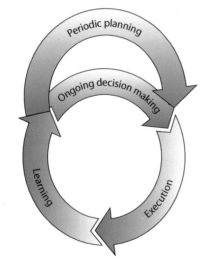

Figure 11.4 The Ongoing Strategy Cycle

often make the decision stronger; multiple people engage in applying strategy, thus deepening their collective sense of the strategies' meaning and application; and more people are prepared, because of their participation in the considerations, to be ambassadors for the decision's implementation. Comparatively, this approach to decision making develops leaders across an organization much more effectively than participation in episodic strategic planning exercises.

Inclusive decision making works when everyone is clear on intended impact and the core organizational strategies being deployed to achieve that impact, which the matrix map process clarifies. Organizational strategies are not programs and services; they are cross-cutting approaches to the work that distinguish your organization's contribution to solving a problem or responding to a community need. Needle exchange is a program; harm reduction is a strategy. Immigration reform advocacy is a program; training and employing undocumented volunteers across all programs is a strategy. Live theater is a program; producing only new works by unknown playwrights is a strategy. An annual fundraising campaign is a program; year-round donor stewardship is a strategy. We keep emphasizing this distinction because we have encountered with so many clients their challenge in making the distinction in their own thinking. Staff and board can make effective decisions together only if they understand and embrace the core strategies used to achieve intended impact.

Inclusive decision making works when everyone is clear on intended impact and the core organizational strategies being deployed to achieve that impact, which the matrix map process clarifies.

In the End: Leadership

The sustainability mindset will not become part of your organization's DNA, as we believe it must, if making it so is not an explicit goal of staff and board leaders. Just as leadership is a process, not a position, sustainability is a mindset—an orientation—that can be cultivated only by engaging everyone in dual-bottom-line thinking, strategy development, and decision making. The great leadership thinkers Margaret Wheatley and Myron Kellner-Rogers described this truth powerfully:

> *Participation is not a choice.* We have no choice but to invite people into the process of rethinking, redesigning, restructuring the organization. We ignore people's need to participate at our own peril. If they're involved, they will create a future that already has them in it.[2]

We know that leaders who take their guidance deeply to heart will make the highest and best use of the matrix map process, using it as a catalyst for the sustainability mindset in all staff and board.

Notes

Chapter 1

1. Jan Masaoka, Jeanne Bell and Steve Zimmerman, *Nonprofit Sustainability* (San Francisco: Jossey-Bass, 2010).
2. Ibid., 13.
3. Jim Collins, *Good to Great and the Social Sectors* (Boulder, CO: Jim Collins, 2005).
4. Dana O'Donovan and Noah Rimland Flower, "The Strategic Plan Is Dead. Long Live Strategy," *Stanford Social Innovation Review*, January 10, 2013. http://www.ssireview.org/blog/entry/the_strategic_plan_is_dead._long_live_strategy
5. *Nonprofit Finance Fund's 2013 State of the Sector* (New York: Nonprofit Finance Fund, March 2013). http://survey.nonprofitfinancefund.org/2013/#respondents,demand,finhealth,actions,gov,data,engagement,perceptions
6. Clara Miller, "Shattering the Myth about Diversified Revenue," *Chronicle of Philanthropy*, September 2, 2010. http://philanthropy.com/blogs/money-and-mission/shattering-the-myth-about-diversified-revenue/26652
7. William Foster and Gail Fine, "How Nonprofits Get Really Big," *Stanford Social Innovation Review*, Spring 2007. http://www.ssireview.org/articles/entry/how_nonprofits_get_really_big
8. Jeanne Bell and Marla Cornelius, *Underdeveloped: A National Study of Challenges Facing Nonprofit Fundraising* (San Francisco: CompassPoint Nonprofit Services and the Evelyn and Walter Haas, Jr. Fund, 2013).
9. Simone Joyaux, "Building a Culture of Philanthropy in Your Organization." http://www.simonejoyaux.com/downloads/CultureOfPhilanthropy.pdf

10. Joan Galon King, "A Culture of Philanthropy: Ten Tips to Ensure Your Organizations Has One." www.ezinearticles.com/?A-Culture-of-Philanthropy:-10-Tips-to-Ensure-Your-Organization-Has-One&id=5532269

11. Dan Pallotta, "The Way We Think about Charity Is Dead Wrong" (2013). www.ted.com/talks/dan_pallotta_the_way_we_think_about_charity_is_dead_wrong.html

12. Bill Schambra, "Why Can't We Get over Overhead?" *Nonprofit Quarterly*, June 10, 2013. http://www.nonprofitquarterly.org/management/22427-why-can-t-we-get-over-overhead.html

13. Building Movement Project, "'Five Percent Shifts' Series" (New York: Building Movement Project, 2013). http://www.buildingmovement.org/blog/entry/five_percent_shifts_seriesh

14. Matthew Forti, "Six Theory of Change Pitfalls to Avoid," *Stanford Social Innovation Review*, May 23, 2012.

15. Management Assistance Group, *Network Leadership Innovation Lab Insights* (Washington, DC: Management Assistance Group, 2013). http://www.managementassistance.org/ht/a/GetDocumentAction/i/23707

Chapter 4

1. Susan Colby, Nan Stone, and Paul Carttar, "Zeroing In on Impact," *Stanford Social Innovation Review*, Fall 2004, 24–33.

Chapter 5

1. Jan Masaoka, Jeanne Bell and Steve Zimmerman, *Nonprofit Sustainability* (San Francisco: Jossey-Bass, 2010).

2. Jim Collins, *Good to Great and the Social Sectors* (Boulder, CO: Jim Collins, 2005).

Chapter 8

1. Jim Collins, *Good to Great and the Social Sectors* (Boulder, CO: Jim Collins, 2005).

Chapter 9

1. Nathalie Laidler-Kylander and Julia Shepard Stenzel, *The Brand IDEA: Managing Nonprofit Brands with Integrity, Democracy, and Affinity* (San Francisco: Jossey-Bass, 2014).
2. For more on innovation, we encourage you to look at the many free tools shared by the Stanford University D-School at https://dschool.stanford.edu/use-our-methods/.

Chapter 11

1. Jim Collins, *Good to Great and the Social Sectors* (Boulder: Jim Collins, 2005).
2. Margaret Wheatley and Myron Kellner-Rogers, "Bringing Life to Organizational Change," *Journal for Strategic Performance Measurement* (April/May 1998).

The Authors

Steve Zimmerman is the principal of Spectrum Nonprofit Services based in Milwaukee, Wisconsin, where he provides training and consulting in the areas of finance and strategy for community-based organizations, foundations, and government agencies throughout the country. He is coauthor of *Nonprofit Sustainability: Making Strategic Decisions for Financial Viability*. He also writes for *Blue Avocado*, an online magazine for nonprofits, and has written for *Nonprofit Quarterly* and BoardSource. Prior to starting Spectrum, he was a projects director with CompassPoint Nonprofit Services. His extensive nonprofit experience includes serving as a chief financial officer, development director, and associate director at nonprofits, where he performed turnarounds resulting in increased financial sustainability and programmatic reach. He is a Certified Public Accountant and earned a BA from Claremont McKenna College and an MBA from Yale University.

Jeanne Bell, MNA, is CEO at CompassPoint—a national, nonprofit leadership and strategy practice based in Oakland, CA. She is the coauthor of *Nonprofit Sustainability: Making Strategic Decisions for Financial Viability* (Jossey-Bass/Wiley) and *Financial Leadership: Guiding Your Organization to*

Long-term Success (Turner). In addition to frequent speaking and consulting on nonprofit strategy, she has co-led a number of national research projects, including *UnderDeveloped: A National Study of the Challenges Facing Nonprofit Fundraising* and *Daring to Lead 2011: A National Study of Nonprofit Executive Leadership*. She is a board member at *The Nonprofit Quarterly* and at the Nonprofit Insurance Alliance of California (NIC).

Index

Printed in the USA
CPSIA information can be obtained
at www.ICGtesting.com
LVHW062348180923

758265LV00009B/8